INFORMAL ENGLISH:

Puncture Ladies, Egg Harbors, Mississippi Marbles, and other Curious Words and Phrases of North America

JEFFREY KACIRK

A TOUCHSTONE BOOK
PUBLISHED BY SIMON & SCHUSTER
NEW YORK   LONDON   TORONTO   SYDNEY

Touchstone
Rockefeller Center
1230 Avenue of the Americas
New York, NY 10020

For information regarding special discounts for bulk purchases,
please contact Simon & Schuster Special Sales at 1-800-456-6798
or business@simonandschuster.com

Designed by Melissa Isriprashad

Manufactured in the United States of America

10   9   8   7   6   5   4   3   2   1

Library of Congress Cataloging-in-Publication Data

Kacirk, Jeffrey.
   Informal English : puncture ladies, egg harbors, Mississippi marbles,
and other curious words and phrases of North America / Jeffrey Kacirk.
     p. cm.
   "A Touchstone Book."
   ISBN 0-7432-5493-7
     1. Americanisms—Dictionaries. 2. English language—United
States—Terms and phrases—Dictionaries. 3. English language—
Canada—Terms and phrases—Dictionaries. 4. English language—
United States—Idioms—Dictionaries. 5. English language—United
States—Slang—Dictionaries. 6. English language—Canada—Idioms—
Dictionaries. 7. English language—Canada—Slang—Dictionaries. 8.
Canadianisms—Dictionaries. I. Title.

PE2835.K33 2005
427'.973'03—dc22
                                    2004065940

ACKNOWLEDGMENTS

It could be said of modern wordsmiths, perhaps as much as for any other group of writers, that they "stand on the shoulders of giants." This book is the result not of my own field-work, but of that of many hundreds of dedicated amateur and professional philologists who patiently ferreted out, organized, distilled, and arranged the expressions they encountered since the seventeenth century. I wish it were possible to present the names of more than the most prominent only and I apologize for omitting those others whose work will nevertheless continue to interest readers. I would also like to salute the people who have helped shape the American dialect with their uniquely spoken words, phrases, pronunciations and cadences.

Specifically, my editor, Amanda Patten, and my agent, Bonnie Solow, made this project possible, guiding it from the realm of fantasy to fruition. A special thank-you goes to my wife, Karen, for her editing assistance and spirited encouragement and to Vincent P. O'Hara Jr. for his assistance with my introduction. Additional thanks go to Gloucestershire native David Mason Williams for helping me to distinguish British words from those primarily used in America.

For allowing me to present excerpts from their copyrighted sources I would like to thank the following organizations: the University of Toronto Press, the University of Chicago Press, the Washington University Press, the University of Oklahoma Press, the University of North Carolina Press, the University of Texas Press, the Oregon Historical Society, and Marshall Macy and his family. I also remain grateful to these organizations for their many services and courtesies or for loans of material: the American Dialect Society, the Marin County Public Library, the San Francisco Public Library, the Ozark Folk Center, and the United States Copyright Office.

Frederick Cassidy and Joan Hall's *Dictionary of American Regional English,* which I highly recommend for its comprehensive treatment of reclusive expressions and developmental background of the American dialect, provided me reliable fact-checking information. In addition, H. L. Mencken's *The American Language* supplied welcome commentary on the development of American English. Allen Walker Read's article, "British Recognition of American Speech in the Eighteenth Century," contributed many useful insights into how American speakers were perceived historically.

INTRODUCTION

The conversations we hear around us are often filled with words and phrases that would be out of place in formal writing. The following collection is a tiny sample of the vernacular expressions that have been used over the last four centuries in North America. I have tried to present a diverse cross section of these gems, drawing from different-size communities and various walks of life ranging from white-collar and blue-collar workers to hoboes. Throughout the gathering and editing process, my focus has been on forgotten and less commonly encountered Americanisms, although some are still used today.

Growing up, I was fortunate to live in a number of linguistically distinct parts of America—Milwaukee, San Diego, New Orleans, and briefly New York and Portland, Oregon—and visited other parts of America's "lower 48" and Canada as time permitted. This serendipitous introduction to North America's cultural diversity planted a seed in me that led roundabout to this book. In Louisiana, such phrases as "like a one-legged man in a behind-kickin' contest," describing a person experiencing difficulties, regularly whetted my appetite for entertaining localisms. Since my interest was piqued in the 1970s, I have enjoyed countless moments just listening to people talk.

Elizabethan English in America?

It is intriguing that more than a few current "Americanisms" originated in Shakespeare's Britain before the first European settlements were founded in America. *Baggage,* for example, a fifteenth-century word used by Shakespeare in *As You Like It* and *The Winter's Tale,* faded in England during the 1700s, leaving most of its duties to *luggage.* Meanwhile, both of these terms thrived among English transplants across the Atlantic. In fact, *baggage* is now found in more than two dozen combinations in America, such as *baggage-car,* and is even used metaphorically in the realm of pop psychology, meaning someone's undesirable habits and attitudes.

Disencourage and many other archaic Anglo terms disappeared in the land of their birth but flourished among British settlers, especially in the Ozarks and Appalachia. These older anachronisms were kept alive along with more recent Briticisms like *fair and square* (used by both Francis Bacon and Oliver Cromwell) and the slang coinages *fib, bamboozle,* and *fun,* which can be found in Francis Grose's 1796 *Dictionary of the Vulgar Tongue.* Americans were roundly ridiculed for their use of these lowbrow terms by British-language commentators who believed these were of Yankee origin. In 1908, for example, English critic Charles Whibley wrote pompously in his *American Sketches:*

> That a country which makes a constant boast of its practical intelligence should delight in long, flat, cumbrous collections of syllables such as *locate, operate, antagonize, transportation, communication,* and

proposition is an irony of civilization. These words, if words they may be called, are hideous to the eye, offensive to the ear, and inexpressive to the mind. They are the base coins of the language. They are put upon the street fresh from the [coin] smasher's den.

But thirteen years later, American linguist Gilbert Tucker rightly refuted these misguided accusations in his own book, *American English*:

Mr. Whibley['s] . . . objection . . . rests on his supposing that they are very recently invented by Americans. . . . The fact is every one of them has been in use in England for decades, all but one of them [*transportation,* c. 1776] for centuries.

The use of barbarous expressions by Americans was only a part of what offended some educated ears. Reporting on one of Abraham Lincoln's state banquets at which he was a guest in 1861, American William Howard Russell was amazed at the discordant variations of English he noticed at this affair. Afterward, he wrote of hearing "a diversity of accent almost as great as if a number of foreigners had been speaking English." Without personally leaping into this divisive fray, I have included what I hope is a provocative and revealing quotation before each of the twenty-six alphabetical groupings of entries to briefly introduce some widely varying British and American attitudes toward the emerging language of the New World.

American English Comes of Age

The tide began to turn during the nineteenth century as the works of Mark Twain and his cohorts and subsequent writers softened the resistance felt by many toward America's words and patterns of speech. Walt Whitman's poetry, the plays of Tennessee Williams and Arthur Miller, and the novels of Twain, John Steinbeck, and Ernest Hemingway, to name a few, all thrust the American dialect before readers. As a partial result, Britons began adopting—or in some cases reclaiming—words from America, especially after "talkies" were introduced in 1927. With the language stigma rapidly disappearing, American filmmakers joined in during the late 1930s and 1940s, first introducing generalized accents for character actors, and later crafting such accent-rich films as *To Kill a Mockingbird* in 1962.

The advent of television provided an opportunity for such early sitcoms as *Amos 'n' Andy* and *The Beverly Hillbillies* to exploit elements of dialect speech, including quaint expressions, pronunciation, and mannerisms. Although the dialogue often evoked laughter at the expense of those they depicted and did so without representing true dialects, this paradigm shift toward lively, if exaggerated, conversation helped pave the way for more serious Hollywood fare. Soon afterward, *Bonnie and Clyde* and *Midnight Cowboy* refined these improvements, followed by *The Godfather* and many others. Today, some movies would sound dull or absurd if the specialized language of their scripts was overlooked.

The original gathering of a minor portion of these entries was done not as an academic pursuit, but as an extension of an individual's employment, or lack thereof. I was surprised to learn that in order to compile his *American Tramp and Underworld Slang,* Godfrey Irwin drew from notes he had jotted during his twenty-year stint as a vagrant. In another instance, George Matsell reformatted vocabulary he had collected from criminals (much of which had been borrowed from British thieves' cant) during his long tenure as police chief of New York City. Likewise, Hyman Goldin and two associates cobbled together the clandestine records of thirty carefully selected "convict-editors" from America's state prison system for their gritty but credible *Dictionary of the American Underworld Lingo.*

The definitions of Noah Webster and his competitor Joseph Worcester are largely absent from these pages because they tended to reject many informalisms in favor of more mainstream English. Most of their entries, while certainly used in normal conversation, were conservative choices that have predictably survived the test of time. Webster's limited interest in American dialect words and slang prompted him to underestimate in 1828 that fewer than fifty words used in America were not also current in England. Although vernacular terms constitute the bulk of my selections, many were also found in fiction and nonfiction writings.

The Boontling Language

Between 1880 and 1920, a community lingo developed in the Anderson Valley of California's rural Mendocino County. In and around Boonville, a patois containing more than a thousand words and phrases came into being that deserves a place among America's most curious subdialects. In the "Boontling" language, the habits, traits and appearances of local residents were preserved in a manner similar to the baseball prowess of Babe Ruth, whose name became synonymous across America with a home run in the 1920s and 1930s. *Blevins,* meaning an inept carpenter (from the name of a family of mediocre tradesmen), is one of several hundred Boont terms that reflects characteristics of valley citizens. Another grouping consists of roughly rehewn phrases such as *bowgley,* a mispronunciation of "big lie." We also find intriguing tidbits like *dom-on-the-saddlehorn,* an expression defined by language researcher Charles Adams as meaning "payment for sexual favors." It seems that a local romance involved a man who would carry on his horse's saddlehorn a dead chicken, or *dom,* as a gift to a woman who savored these fowls.

Notes on the Text

My aim has been to encourage the appreciation of colorful and often neglected expressions in part by reducing the unnecessary detail that some readers associate with books on language. To this end, I opted for a less cluttered and more readable format, with a minimum of dates, footnotes, small print, and cryptic abbreviations. These entries are presented verbatim because I feel that just as Renaissance music is more enjoyable when played on authentic instruments, old expressions often contain more subtle nuances when explained by earlier field linguists, who could then be properly credited for their valuable work.

Where multiple definitions of a term were available, I did not necessarily select the oldest but tried to present the most clear, concise, and thought-provoking descriptions and in some cases combined two or more. A small minority of entries needed to be edited lightly for clarity or in order to add brief notes regarding their origins, but their contents have remained substantially unaltered.

The times of usage I supplied for entries are not intended to be precise. The dates found in my bibliography offer only a sense of when these accumulations were first published, which was sometimes a decade or more after some of the entries were collected. Beyond this it is possible, or even likely, that a fair number of the entries in these source works had been used for decades before being recorded, and some may still be in circulation. So what might seem like an authoritative date could easily prove otherwise. But in general, these dates may serve as a reasonable chronological orientation.

Likewise, the locations mentioned for most of these expressions should suggest only a likely cradle of their gestation rather than an overall distribution. I sometimes wish that these unpredictable terms were found in more orderly geographic confines. But especially with the growth of mass media, former localisms have strayed from their places of origin, making them difficult to account for despite improvements in data compilation. Therefore the reader should consider place references as merely rough snapshots of where terms were recorded. Even so, I should add that as late as the mid–twentieth century, a few American "elocutionists" earned their livings at county fairs by listening to people speak and then guessing—often with surprising accuracy—where the speaker had grown up.

The Future of Amerenglish

It is seldom easy to predict whether a fledgling term will survive. In 1810, the *Massachusetts Spy* weighed in on an ill-fated word that meant "the art of quizzing," declaring, "*Quizzism* is certainly a very good-looking word, and may in time become a popular one." What can be said is that a small percentage of today's outpouring of new words will become respectable. Just as the mainstream nouns *bindery, lobbyist, gunslinger,* and *doughnut* began as questionable American coinages, and *lengthy* as simply a corruption of *length,* the modern slang expressions *sitcom, micromanage,* and *silver bullet* seem to be here to stay. But what about the

New Englandism *blowdown,* a description of fallen limbs and leaves after a storm? Although never really popular in its heyday a century ago, *blowdown* perhaps sounded a bit more dignified than some others and had a four-hundred-year-old synonym in *windfall,* yet its use dwindled over time.

Colloquialisms, such as a favorite of mine, the now widely distributed ambiguity "I don't guess," can add home-grown charm to even the most mundane conversation. Often containing an abundance of metaphor, simile, and common sense, these distillations of practical experience are easily bandied about by those whose education has not displaced their native intelligence. Despite ongoing cultural homogenization, surprising numbers of spicy folk extractions will surely live on in every region of North America, displaying a blend of homespun wisdom and humor. I hope the expressions to follow will make those spoken around you easier to notice and more enchanting. So "make long arms!" as has often been said in the Northeast to invite dinner guests to help themselves.

It is easy to foresee that in no very distant period their language will become as independent of England as they themselves are; and altogether as unlike English as the Dutch or Flemish is unlike German, or the Norwegian unlike the Danish, or the Portuguese unlike Spanish.

—Reverend Jonathan Boucher, English-born philologist, Virginia resident, and compiler of the *Glossary of Archaic and Provincial* [American] *Words*, writing on American English in 1777

above snakes

Above the ground. [Tucker]

abskise

To depart, go away. Of local usage in parts of the West settled by Germans; probably [from] German *abscheiden*. [Clapin]

ackempucky

Any food mixture of unknown ingredients. West Virginia. [Wentworth]

acknowledge the corn

A confession of having been mistaken or outwitted. . . . A popular account of the origin of the phrase ascribes it to the misfortunes of a flatboatman who had come down to New Orleans with two flatboats laden, one with corn, the other with potatoes. He was tempted to enter a gambling establishment, and lost his money and his produce. On returning at night to the wharf, he found his boat with corn had sunk in the river, and when the winner came next morning to demand the stake he received the answer, "Stranger, I *acknowledge the corn*—take it. But the potatoes you *can't* have." [Schele de Vere]

ackruffs

River-thieves; river-pirates. [Matsell]

across lots

To go *across lots* is to proceed by the shortest route; similarly to do anything in the most expeditious manner. The phrase had its rise in the natural tendency of settlers in thinly populated districts to shorten the distance from point to point by leaving the road and striking [out] across vacant lots. Brigham Young familiarized its idiomatic use in the notorous saying "We'll send the Gentiles to hell *across lots*." [Farmer]

admiral's room

In the seventeenth and eighteenth centuries, the skipper of the English fishing vessel arriving first in a [Newfoundland] harbor in the spring was the "Fishing Admiral" for the season. He had his choice of location of fishing room; hence our expression. [Sandilands]

after night

After night is a local expression, peculiar to Pennsylvania and some of the border[ing] states, where night is very commonly used for the hours of the afternoon; hence, "Court will be open again *after night*" simply means *after candlelight* [becomes necessary], as it is expressed every-where else. [Schele de Vere]

airtights

Canned goods. Today we can buy anything in cans, from pie-dough to potato strings. But the open-range cowboy rarely saw any canned foods other than corn, tomatoes, peaches, and milk. West. [R. Adams]

Alabama wool

Cotton [for] clothing, especially underwear. Pacific North-west. [McCulloch]

alarm-lock

A lock, padlock, bolt, latch, or knob so arranged that a bell is caused to ring by any movement of its parts, or by any attempt to open the door . . . to which it is fastened. [Whitney]

Albany beef

[A] mixture of sailors' names and landsmen's notions has led to the cant terms by which sturgeons and herrings are apt to be known on shore. The former, coming up the Hudson River as far as Albany, and being highly esteemed there, especially when roasted in the form of steaks, are popularly known as *Albany beef*; the herring, caught in abundance near Taunton in the state of Massachusetts, is called there a *Taunton turkey,* half in derision and half, no doubt, for the sake of the alliteration. [Schele de Vere] *New York turkey,* bacon. . . . *Arkansas chicken,* salt pork. Northwest Arkansas. [Carr]

allerickstix

Presumably a corruption of German *alles richtig.* Used in common schools of Cincinnati as equivalent for the English *all right.* "How did you get through examination? *Allerickstix.*" [Hart]

all horns and rattles

Said of one displaying a fit of temper. A man in this mood, as one cowboy said, "maybe don't say nothin', but it ain't safe to ask questions." West. [R. Adams]

all-overs

Nervous jimjams, creeps, fidgets. "I don't like such stories. They give me the *all-overs.*" Eastern Alabama. [Payne]

all sorts

The drippings of glasses in saloons, collected and sold at half-price to drinkers who are not overly particular. [Clapin] "A counter perforated in elaborately-pricked patterns, like a convivial shroud, apparently for ornament, but ready for the purpose of allowing the drainings, overflowings, and outspillings of the . . . . glasses to drop through which, being collected with sundry washings, and a dash, perhaps, of fresh material is, by the thrifty landlord, dispensed to his customers under the title of *all sorts.*" [Sala]

all turkey

"It's *all turkey,*" a quaint saying indicating that it's all equally good. It is said that an old gentleman who was asked at a Thanksgiving dinner if he preferred white meat or dark replied, "I don't care which—it's *all turkey.*" [Barrère]

ambeer

Tobacco juice; the spittle produced by chewing tobacco. Virginia. [Green] *Ambia* [is] used in the South and West for tobacco juice. It is a euphemism for the spittle produced by this voluntary ptyalism. More commonly spelled and pronounced *ambeer,* probably from *amber,* denoting its color. [Bartlett]

amen corner

Seats near the pulpit in church. Southeastern Missouri.

[Crumb] That part of a meeting-house occupied by persons who assist the preacher with occasional and irregular responses. [Thornton]

American tweezers

An ingenious instrument of American invention by means of which it is possible to turn a key in a door and unlock it from the outside. [Farmer]

among the willows

Said of one dodging the law. West. [R. Adams] *Keep close to the willows,* to be conventional, conservative, modest. Nude boys, swimming in willow-bordered creeks, keep close to the trees to avoid being seen. Ozarks. [Randolph & Wilson]

Anglo-bluenose

A Nova Scotian. [Scargill] From the species of potato which [Nova Scotians] produce and claim to be the best in the world. [Johnson] *White nose,* a man spending his first winter in Newfoundland. [England]

ant-bed

An ant-hill. Eastern Alabama. [Payne]

anxious mourner, anxious bench

Persons who are peculiarly excited to a consciousness of their sinfulness and the necessity of seeking salvation are called *anxious mourners,* and are led to the *anxious bench.* [Schele de Vere] *Mourner's bench,* a seat for "mourners" near the pulpit. Southern Indiana. [Hanley]

apperflappety

Willingness or obligingness. Nebraska. [Pound]

apple-palsy

Plain drunk, caused by too much [apple-]jack. Burlington County, New Jersey. [Lee]

apple-palsy

Arkansas wedding cake

Corn bread. Pacific Northwest. [McCulloch]

Arkansayan

A compromise form between *Arkansawyer* and *Arkansan*. *Arkansawyer*, both as a noun and as an adjective, is universal among the uneducated and occurs even among the educated. The adjective and the noun *Arkansan* are in disrepute among the uneducated and others because the word suggests *Kansan*. Kansas and Kansans are very unpopular in Arkansas. [Carr]

armsweep

The length of reach or swing of the arm. [Lyons]

Armstrong mower

A hand scythe; similarly of other hand-operated tools. [Weseen]

arm waitress

A waitress skilled at piling dishes on her arm. "Experienced *arm waitress* wanted." —*Seattle Times* want-ad. [Garrett]

astern the lighter

Tardy, lagging behind; a lighter being a slow-moving craft

used for transferring cargo. To be *astern the lighter* is to be rather a laggard, and the term is used in a contemptuous sense, as "Oh, he's always *astern the lighter*." Nantucket. [Macy]

at liberty

Unemployed. An actor without a job is *at liberty*. Theater slang. [Weseen]

at oneself

Up to one's full strength or ability. "I can easily pick 300 pounds of cotton when I am *at myself*." Eastern Alabama. [Payne]

attitudinize

To assume affected attitudes, airs, or postures. [Worcester]

Attleborough

Not genuine; made to imitate. At the town of Attleborough [Massachusetts] jewelry is manufactured from the baser metals, or so alloyed as to deceive those who are not good judges of the genuine article. [Matsell]

autospill

An emptying of an automobile by tilting or overturning. Kansas. [Ruppenthal]

axe-craft, axery

The art of felling trees. [Thornton]

azzle

To back out. "We made a fair trade but he *azzled* out of it." Southeastern Missouri. [Crumb]

Americanisms . . . have long been a bugbear to purists, the despair of etymologists, and an unfailing source of wonder, amusement, and in many respects a puzzle to the general reader. To the student of comparative philology, however, a large number of these words, phrases, and colloquialisms, which at first sight seem novel, uncouth, and obscene are, when scrutinised, found to possess a parentage that cannot be questioned.

—Englishman John S. Farmer, in the preface to his
Americanisms Old and New (1889)

back-cap

"To give a *back-cap*" is thieves' argot meaning to expose one's past life. In Mark Twain's *Life on the Mississippi*, a pretended converted thief is made to say, "I told him all about my being in prison and . . . didn't fear no one giving me a *back-cap* and running me off the job." [Farmer]

backlings

A grade of whisky intermediate in strength between "first shot" [the strongest] and "singlings" [the weakest]. Eastern Kentucky. [Shearin]

back number

A person who, like a back [issue] of a magazine or periodical, has had his day and is no longer in demand. Western Canada. [Sandilands]

back teeth's a-floatin'

To express painful fullness of the bladder. Snake County, Missouri. [Taylor]

bad row of stumps

"He is in a *bad row of stumps*" means to be in trying places; from the trouble one has in plowing stumpy land. Kentucky. [Fruit]

bait can

A dinner pail or lunch basket; [from] *bait,* a meal, usually a light lunch. Ozarks. [Randolph]

bakehead

A locomotive fireman, since many railroaders claim these workers are none too bright merely because of the intense heat they face while firing their engines. The term is also applied to stokers of any boiler or engine, and has become fairly common as a substitute for *fool* or *idiot,* especially among migratory workers. [Irwin]

baker's fog

Disparaging term for commercially produced bread. Newfoundland. [Story]

balditute

A state of baldness. "Trouble has brung these gray hairs and this premature *balditude.*" —Mark Twain's *Huckleberry Finn.* [Farmer]

bamsquabbled

This coined word, which is, however, rarely used except in humorous writings, first saw the light in *The Legend of the American War.* It signifies discomfiture and defeat, or stupefaction; sometimes written *bumsquabbled.* [Farmer]

bangbellies

Pancakes made of flour, fat [often from seals], and molasses, fried on a pan. Newfoundland. [Devine]

bango

A Negro expletive without any special meaning, except one of general pleasure. It is frequently heard, and is common to the black race throughout the States and the West Indies. [Farmer]

banjolin

An instrument that combines characteristics of the banjo and the mandolin. *Banjolele,* an instrument that combines characteristics of the banjo and ukulele. [Weseen]

barb wire garters

Those who get no special honors or decorations are said to be awarded the *barb wire garters*. Soldiers' slang. [Weseen]

barfoot tea

A very curious term is connected with the fondness of Western men for coffee and tea: "I take my tea *barfoot*," said a backwoodsman when asked if he would take cream and sugar. [Schele de Vere]

barfoot tea

barked pie

Pie with an upper as well as a lower crust, such as apple, raisin, and mince. *Open-face pie,* pie with only an under-crust, such as custard, lemon, and chocolate. [Weseen]

baseballist

A baseball player. [Thornton]

basket-meetings

Occasionally, after the peculiar manner of the pilgrim fathers, religious exercises are quaintly mixed up with work and fun. A corn-husking is announced or a raising-bee is arranged, and the neighbors from far and near assemble, each bringing his provisions in a basket. From the latter feature these picnics derive their names of *basket-meetings.* The most determined polemic divine, however, could hardly venture upon a long harangue there, since the minds are bent upon hard work and gay frolic, the means of escape are open on all sides and the tempting baskets at any moment ready to allure the audience away from every thought. [Schele de Vere]

basket of chips

A metaphor for a pleasant appearance; perhaps because a supply of chips gives promise of a good fire. [Thornton]

battlin' bench

A bench, board, log-end, or the like where clothes are *battled* in washing. Appalachia. [Dingus] *Battling-stick,* a paddle used in washing clothes. Instead of using a washboard, the clothes are laid on an inclined smooth board and beaten with a *battling-stick*. Southeastern Missouri. [Crumb]

bean day

A day when fishermen catch no fish and must eat beans as a substitute. Martha's Vineyard, Massachusetts. [Rees]

bean-water

"Up on one's *bean-water*," feeling very lively, strong, frisky. "I'm right up on my *bean-water* this morning." Maine, northern New Hampshire. [England]

beast-back

Horseback. "I went *beast-back* to town." Kentucky. [Fruit]

bee-bread

The pollen of flowers collected by bees as food for their young. [Webster] A plant much visited by bees, or cultivated for their use, as red clover. [Whitney]

beef straight

When a man has nothing but beef for a meal, and must eat it without bread, vegetables, &c., it is *beef straight*. [Barrère]

beeves

The plural [of *beef*, a single ox] occurs in the American vernacular. [Thornton]

behaving party

They had been at what [in New Orleans] are very significantly termed "behaving parties." In these, the persons present are supposed to be on their good behavior. [Flint]

bellmare

A horse chosen to lead a caravan or drove of mules in the Southwest. This is the familiar *bellmare* who, in slang language, gives her name to the leader of political parties. [Schele de Vere]

Belsnickel

A masked and hideously disguised person who goes from house to house on Christmas eve, beating—or pretending to beat—the children and servants and throwing down nuts and cakes before leaving. A noisy party accompanies him, often with a bell, which has influenced the English name. [From] German *pelz,* a pelt, skin with hair, as a bear skin, here used as a disguise, and perhaps associated with *peltzen,* to pelt, and *nickel,* nix, in the sense of a demon. Pennsylvania Dutch. [Haldeman]

bend the fists

That is, double them. Portsmouth, New Hampshire. [Allen]

berdache

From the evidence available, the word means *hermaphrodite* when applied to animals, but *homosexual* when applied to man. Among Missouri French today, the word means *coward.* Mississippi Valley. [McDermott]

best bib and tucker

One's finest clothes. Central New York, New England, Philadelphia, and Missouri. [White]

bettermost

Best. Central Connecticut. [Mead]

betting his eyes

A term used by gamblers when a "sucker" looks on at a game but does not bet. [Matsell]

between the jigs and the reels

During odd times. [It] has another meaning akin to the expression *what with one thing and another.* "So, *between the jigs and the reels,* poor Tom lost all his money." In an expression of determination, the phrase may mean *somehow.* "I'll do it *between the jigs and the reels.*" Newfoundland. [Devine]

bibibles

Food of liquid kind; an innovation formed on the model of *edibles,* which has little to recommend it, save its vulgarity. [Farmer]

bible-backed

Round-shouldered or hump-backed. [Thornton]

bide a wee

Stay a while. Cape Fear, North Carolina. [Steadman]

big church

No church; used facetiously to indicate that one is not a member of any church or denomination. "I belong to the *big church*." Eastern Alabama. [Payne]

big dog of the tanyard

The name often given to an overbearing person who will allow no one else to speak or differ from his views. The bold figure of speech is derived from the fact that tanyards are generally guarded by fierce bulldogs. [Schele de Vere]

bigging it

Exaggerating. North Carolina. [Cooper]

biggity

Consequential; giving oneself airs; a negro term. [Farmer]

big jump

The cowman's reference to death. When one died, he was said to have *taken the big jump,* and a good many cowmen were "weighted down with their boots." West. [R. Adams]

bingle

A coin of base metal, value ten cents, used for gambling. Sierra County, California. [Lehman]

bird-line view

A bird's-eye view. Massachusetts. [Thornton]

blackberry baby

An illegitimate child; also *blackberry patch baby*. Northwestern Arkansas. [Wentworth]

blackberry storm

A storm said to occur when blackberries are in season.

Blackberry winter, a season of relatively low temperature when blackberries are in blossom. Northwest Arkansas. [Carr]

black-coat

A common and familiar name for a clergyman, as *red-coat* is for a [British] soldier. [Worcester]

black-coat

black diamonds

Coal. Kansas, Pennsylvania, Nebraska. [Ruppenthal]

black dishes

Cooking utensils, by contrast with glass and china. "I will leave the *black dishes* for her to clean." Kansas. [Ruppenthal]

Black Dutch

Dark Pennsylvania mountain people, probably of Near Eastern or aboriginal stock. Central Pennsylvania. [Shoemaker]

black riding

At the college of South Carolina, it has until within a few years been customary for the students, disguised and painted black, to ride across the college-yard at midnight on horseback, with vociferations and the sound of horns. *Black riding* is recognized by the laws of the college as a very high offence, punishable with expulsion. [Hall]

blackwash

To magnify defects and give prominence to them. [Weseen]

blanket order

A wholesale order which, to make up the bulk required to bring it within the scope of special terms, permits the merchant some license to fill up with an assortment of other saleable goods very similar to the kind first specified. Western Canada. [Sandilands]

bleenie

A frankfurter. Eastern Iowa. [Wentworth]

blenker

To plunder. A cant phrase much used during the Civil War. Possibly allied to the northern provincialism *blenk,* a trick or stratagem. [Farmer & Henley]

blind-buck and Davy

A clumsy, weak-sighted, stumbling person. Central Pennsylvania. [Shoemaker]

blind eel

Among fishermen, "to catch a *blind eel*" is to bring to the surface a piece of seaweed or some other worthless object in place of the fish supposed to have been hooked. Metaphorically the expression signifies obtaining a result of little worth compared with that sought. [Farmer]

blinky-john

Milk just beginning to sour. Southern Illinois. [Rice]

blonde-bound

Held up by a woman; an excuse for being late on the job. Pacific Northwest. [McCulloch]

bloviate

To talk aimlessly and boastingly; to indulge in high fa-
lutin'. [Farmer & Henley]

blowed in the glass

Genuine; to be trusted. From the old-time liquor bottles
and other containers which had the name of the maker or
the product blown in the glass to insure the quality. A
"blowed in the glass stiff" then is one who never works,
one in the know and able to take care of himself in any
situation. [Irwin]

bluebacks

The paper money of the Confederates. A cant name originating, as in the case of United States paper currency
greenbacks, in the colour of the printing on the reverse.
[Farmer & Henley] *Redback,* one of the treasury notes issued by the Republic of Texas in 1838. . . . Called from
the color of the paper. [Craigie]

Blue Hen's Chickens

A slang name for the inhabitants of Delaware. Captain
Caldwell, an officer of the first Delaware regiment in
the American War of Independence, was known for
his love of cock-fighting. Being personally popular, and
his regiment becoming famous for their valour, they
were soon known as "game-cocks"; and as Caldwell
maintained that no cock was truly game unless its
mother was a blue hen, his regiment and subsequently
Delawareans generally, became known as Blue Hen's
Chickens, and Delaware as the Blue Hen State. [Farmer
& Henley]

blue John

Milk deficient in butter fat, or in richness, so that it is of
bluish color. Nebraska, Louisiana. [Ruppenthal]

bluelights

Traitors. [Tucker] Even generations afterward when the inhabitants of the Land of Steady Habits [Connecticut] were accused of having made signals along the coast for the benefit of the British during the War of 1812, these lights . . . were called *blue lights,* adding a new word to the vocabulary of treason. The charge, it is said, was utterly unfounded, but the term has survived to this day and is frequently used in political controversies. [Schele de Vere] At the University of Vermont this term is used . . . to designate "a boy who sneaks about college and reports to the faculty of the shortcomings of his fellow students." [Hall] *Blue-light men,* a term of reproach used by the Democrats against the Federalists. [Fearon]

board round

A term little heard now but once very common. . . . In the rural districts of New England, a schoolteacher, instead of receiving tuition fees from parents of the children whom he taught, would be *boarded round* in rotation among those indebted to him. [Farmer] *Boarding around* became a term for having no home, and it is still heard in such a sentence as, "Mother sold the old place after Dad went, and now she's *boarding 'round.*" Maine. [Gould]

board with Aunt Polly

To draw insurance for sickness or accident. *Ride polly,* to draw half pay as a result of an accident. Miners and loggers. [Weseen]

boatable

Navigable with boats; a useful word. [Dunglison] This word is rarely used by Americans, and never by Englishmen in writing. A correspondent, however, remarks that "in very familiar discourse it is perhaps used among some of the

English, but it has scarcely a right to be called a classical word." [Pickering] *Boatable* . . . originated in America but proved so useful that it has found its way into English dictionaries. [Schele de Vere]

body and breeches

Altogether; entirely. A decidedly colloquial expression. [Thornton]

boette

A female hobo. [Weseen] The number of women who take to the road each year has been estimated as high as eighty thousand. [Related to] *bohobo,* a young hobo, and *boes' park,* the railway yards; *bo* [is] a contraction of *hobo;* the plural *boes* is applied to tramps as well. [Kane]

boffo

A dollar. One year. "Old John is in prison [for] fifteen *boffos.*" [Goldin]

boggering

The act of nodding, beckoning; a challenge. [From Irish] *bagraim,* I beckon, I threaten. Newfoundland. [Story]

boil up

To wash and boil the clothing, the latter to kill vermin. The true hobo . . . welcomes any opportunity to keep his person clean and neat, since a good front is essential in looking for work. [Irwin]

bone dish

A narrow, curved dish meant to fit close to a dinner plate, its purpose being to provide a place of disposal for bones and other inedible bits. In the nineteenth century, a really fine set of china always included bone dishes. New England. [Haywood]

bone-orchard

To most vagabonds, the material things of life far out-

weigh any other considerations, and the one crop a graveyard may be depended on to yield is certainly bones.
[Irwin] *Boneyard,* cemetery. [Farmer]

boof
Peach brandy. In Westerwaldish, *buff* is cider-water—
cider made by wetting the pomace and pressing it a second time. Pennsylvania Dutch. [Haldeman]

booklegger
A person who deals in forbidden books; a book dealer
who follows unfair practices. [Weseen]

bookwright
A writer of books; an author; a term of slight contempt.
[Lyons]

bossy in a bowl
Beef stew; from Latin *bos,* an ox. [Irwin]

Bostonian
It was indeed by the name of *Bostonians* that all Americans were known in France. . . . Coffee-houses took that
name, and a game invented at that time, played with
cards, was called *Boston,* and is to this day [1830] exceedingly fashionable at Paris by that appellation. [Breck]

bought his thumb
When an old-timer said, "I bought his thumb," he meant
that he suspicioned the storekeeper rested his thumb on the
scale when weighing the meat, cheese, or turnips, a proce-
dure good for two or three more ounces on the dial and a
few cents more on the price. New England. [Haywood]

box of teeth
An accordion; [also] *bricklayer's piano, groan-box,
pleated piano, stomach Steinway, to-and-fromie.* [Berrey]

box social
A social event at which boxes—often decorated with

colored paper and ribbons—of food are offered at auction to male bidders, the successful bidder having the privilege of eating and dancing with the woman who prepared the lunch. [Scargill]

bran dance

A Western dance at which the ground is generally sprinkled with Indian meal. [Thornton]

brass-toes

Brass-toed shoes worn by children; also called *copper-toes*. Eastern Alabama. [Payne]

breachy

This is a common word among the farmers of New England in speaking of oxen that are unruly and apt to break through their enclosures. [Pickering]

bread-bag

The stomach. [Matsell]

break the road

The person *breaks the road* who is first to pass over the road after a snowstorm. Nebraska. [Pound]

bred-stuff

All kinds of flour, meal, farinaceous substances, grain. In England, *corn* is used as the generic term. In America, *corn* is always meant to apply to maize—otherwise called Indian corn—the most abundant and useful vegetable production in the United States. [Humphreys] *Breadstuffs,* one of the most useful words in the language for which we have to thank our American cousins. Its introduction [by Thomas Jefferson] goes back over a hundred years. [Farmer] In Jamaica, the term *bread-kind* is applied to esculent roots, &c. substituted for bread. [Bartlett]

breeze of luck

A period of prosperity, good luck. "I now began to think

we had struck a *breeze of luck.*" —Davy Crockett's *Autobiography,* 1834. [Craigie]

bricketty

Irritable. [Thornton]

brick in the hat

A drunken man is said to have a *brick in the hat,* the allusion being to top-heaviness and inability to preserve a steady gait. [Farmer]

brick watch

Used when the speaker is sure of something. "You can bet a *brick watch* I did." Southwestern Wisconsin. [Savage]

briggle

To busy oneself without purpose. Western Indiana. [Brown] *Briggler,* one who attempts but never finishes anything; a trifler. Central Pennsylvania. [Shoemaker]

broad alley

The middle passage of a meeting-house or a church. [Thornton] *Alley-way,* long hall in a house. Maine. [Maxfield]

broken dose

A little at a time. "I always give quinine in *broken doses.*" Southeastern Missouri. [Crumb]

broomed

A schooner was *broomed* when the owner wanted to sell her. Instead of an ad in the paper, as in modern times, the old birch broom used in sweeping the deck was hoisted to the mast-head. Newfoundland. [Devine]

brosh

Brittle; [from] Dutch *brós,* frail. A New York word. [Barrère]

brought on

Not homemade. "The clothes you have on I see are *brought on.*" Tennessee. [Edson]

brought up in a sawmill

Applied to a person who forgets to close the door in cold weather, since the older type of saw mill had no doors. Western New York. [Bowen] "What did you leave the door open for? Were you *brought up in a sawmill?*" Hampstead, New Hampshire. [Carr]

Bryn-Mawrtyr

A woman who has been connected with Bryn Mawr College as an undergraduate. [Savage]

bubbly-jock

A turkey gobbler. Central Pennsylvania. [Shoemaker]

buck-darting

A zigzag method of sailing employed on tidewater creeks. New Jersey. [Lee]

buck fever

Agitation of an inexperienced deer hunter. [Bartlett]

Buckle of the Wheat Belt

A euphemistic name given to Winnipeg because of its preponderating trade, but other cities quite centrally situated on the great Canadian wheat belt also claim the title. Western Canada. [Sandilands]

buck-party

Buck-party, like *stag-party,* denotes a company without ladies. [Schele de Vere] *Gander-party,* a social gathering of men only. [Lowell] *Hen-party,* a party to which women only are invited. Eastern Alabama. [Payne] *Stag-dance,* a dance performed by males only, in bar-rooms, &c. Also called a *bull-dance.* [Bartlett]

buck the tiger

To gamble; derived from the parti-coloured divisions or stripes on a gambling table. [Barrère]

buffalo cider

The ludicrous name given to the liquid in the stomach of the buffalo, which the thirsty hunter drinks when he has killed his game at a great distance from the water. *Prairie-bitters,* a horrible mixture of water and buffalo-gall, to which great medicinal powers are ascribed by hunters and border-settlers. [Schele de Vere]

bugsarn

Interjection expressing annoyance or exasperation. "*Bugsarn* it! It's going to rain." Nebraska. [Pound]

bulk and file

Two pickpockets operating together. The *bulk* jostles the party that is to be robbed, and the *file* steals the treasure. [Matsell]

bull-cook

A male cook at a mining or lumber camp. Pacific Northwest. [Lehman]

bull fiddle

A bass viol. Aroostook County, Maine. [Carr] *Bull-fiddle voice,* deep bass voice. [Berrey]

bulrusher

A foundling; an illegitimate child; anyone whose lineage is not immediately known or traceable. Biblical allusion to the discovery of Moses in the bulrushes. Boontling language. [C. Adams]

bum-sick

Inimical to all vagrants; applied to those towns and cities which have had too many tramps and beggars to feed, and which are heartily tired of all such characters. [Irwin]

bumswizzled

Used in "I'll be *bumswizzled*." Nebraska. [Pound] *Gums-*

wizzled, exclamation expressing annoyance or surprise. "I'll be *gumswizzled!*" Nebraska. [Pound]

bundle of brooms

In the expression "I didn't know him from a *bundle of brooms,*" I did not recognize him by sight. Similarly used are *bag of meal* and *basket of chips.* New York. [Monroe]

bundling

A man and woman lying on the same bed with their clothes on; an expedient practised in America on a scarcity of beds where, on such occasions, husbands and parents frequently permitted travellers to bundle with their wives and daughters. [Grose] Among other hideous customs, the Yankees attempted to introduce that of *bundling,* which Dutch lasses . . . seemed very well inclined to follow. [Irving] Notwithstanding the great modesty of the females . . . it would be accounted the greatest . . . piece of civility to ask her to *bundle,* a custom as old as the first settlement in 1634. Connecticut. [Peters]

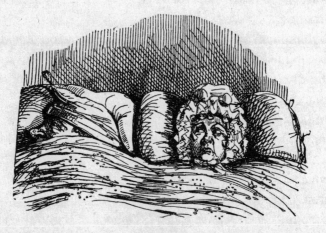

bundling

JEFFREY KACIRK

bun-duster

A small-salaried male who frequents teas and other entertainments and never makes any efforts to repay his social obligations. Otherwise, a "cake-eater." Bryn Mawr College. [Savage]

bungersome

Clumsy. Virginia. [Green]

bungfunger

To startle; to confuse. Also used as an adjective for *confounded*. [Farmer & Henley]

Bungtown

An imaginary town in New England, so called from the slang term *bung,* meaning to lie. Hence, *Bungtown copper* is a favorite name of the spurious English half-penny, which has no currency in th[is] country. It is said that such a coin was really once made—a counterfeit, of course—in a town then bearing the name Bungtown, but since then known as Rehoboth, in Massachusetts. [Schele de Vere]

bunkumsquint

Excellent. "That looks *bunkumsquint.*" Nebraska. [Louise Pound]

burnsides

A style . . . such as that affected by General Burnside (1824–1881) consisting of a moustache, whiskers, and a clean-shaven chin. [Thornton]

bush-bacon

A rabbit. East Texas. [Wentworth]

bush-nipple

A woodsman or hermit. Central Pennsylvania. [Shoemaker]

bush up

To hide in the shrubbery. Ozarks. [Randolph]

busy as a cranberry merchant

Exceedingly busy. [Carr]

butterine

Of American origin, but now equally applied in England, to a spurious kind of butter composed of fatty substances other than cream; also called *oleo-margarine,* margarine, etc. The sale of these products for butter is now prohibited by law in England, except distinctly sold under their true names and character, while in America even restaurant keepers are required to make public announcement if they use the article. [Farmer]

buttermilk cow

A bull. When children ask why a bull is not milked, they are told that he is a "buttermilk cow." Western Indiana. [Brown] *Bull* is used by Americans in good society only as a financial term connected with "bears." . . . It is commonly believed that *ox* is the only respectable term by which a bull can be safely designated, and even "gentleman-cow" has been attempted by bashful prudes. There is a story . . . that a gray-headed American gentleman was seen to doff his hat reverently and apologize to a clergyman for having inadvertently used in his presence the plain Saxon term. [Schele de Vere] *Top cow, he thing, male cow, duke, cow's husband,* a bull. [Berrey] Ozarkers say *male, cow-critter, brute,* or *cow-brute.* [Randolph & Wilson]

buttock down

Sit down. North Carolina. [Cooper]

buttonhole relation

A third or fourth cousin, at least; somebody distantly related but not close enough to bother about. Sometimes a family friend who is no kin at all, but is held dear. Similar to *woodpile cousin* . . . like a *buttonhole relation* but less likely to mean actual blood connections. Maine. [Gould]

butzo

Watch out! Run! [Goldin]

by scissors!

A mild oath. Eastern Maine. [Chase] *Hell and scissors!* A peculiar interjection signifying that while one [is] startled at something, there is something ridiculous in the affair. [Barrère]

If, in an assemblage of a hundred educated, well-bred people—
one half of them from London, Oxford, and Liverpool, and the
other from Boston, New York, and Philadelphia—a ready and
accurate phonographer were to take down every word spoken
during an evening's entertainment, I feel quite sure that it
would be impossible to distinguish in his printed report the
speech of the Britons from that of the Americans, except by the
possible occurrence of acknowledged local slang. . . . I am
strongly inclined to the opinion that . . . there would be somewhat more slang heard from the British than from the American half of the company, and also a greater number of free
and easy deviations from correct English.

—American Shakespearean scholar
Richard Grant White's *Words and Their Uses* (1870)

C & A pocket
A pocket with the bottom cut out so that the whole inner
lining of the coat serves as a larger pocket of immense carrying capacity. Certain hick jurists still regard the posses-
sion of a coat with *C & A pockets* as prima facie evidence
that the wearer is a tramp. [Kane]

cablegram
An Americanism for *telegram*. [Johnson]

cadulix
Male genital organ. Central Pennsylvania. [Shoemaker]

calf-rope

A signal of surrender. "I'll make him say *calf-rope*." Eastern Alabama. [Payne]

calf-skin fiddle

A drum. [Matsell]

calf-skin fiddle

Calgary Redeye

A mixture of tomato juice and beer, a drink associated with Calgary and the surrounding area. [Scargill]

calibogus

A very old name for a mixture of rum and spruce beer, being quoted by [Francis] Grose in 1785 as "an American beverage." The last two syllables of the word are thought to be derived from the French *bagasse,* the refuse of the sugar cane. This view would seem to be supported by the fact that rum is itself a product of the sugar cane. [Farmer & Henley]

California blanket

Newspapers used for sleeping purposes. *Bum's comforter,* newspapers. [Weseen] So called since much of the southern part of the state has a climate which allows of sleeping out of doors with but scant covering. [Irwin]

California widow

A married woman whose husband is away from her for any extended period; a *grass-widow* in the least offensive sense of that term. The expression dates from the period of the California gold fever, when so many men went West, leaving their wives and families behind them. [Farmer]

callahooting

Careening along at a breakneck pace. Central Pennsylvania. [Shoemaker]

called to straw

In some parts of the Ozark region *straw* means childbirth. A woman who is *called to straw* is about to have a baby. I first assumed that it referred to a straw mattress, just as "hit the hay" signifies "go to bed." But many natives, including physicians and midwives at widely separated points in Missouri and Arkansas, assure me that *straw* means the act of parturition. . . . It is sometimes used as a verb, as in the sentence "Mable's a-*strawin'* right now." [Randolph & Wilson]

call one's jawbone

To live on credit. Canadian. [Barrère]

call your name

Used in the expression "What do you *call your name*?" meaning "What is your name?" Northwest Arkansas. [Carr]

canvas opera

A circus. [Weseen]

cap the climax

To surpass everything. Central Connecticut. [Mead]

caracoly

A mixture of gold, silver, and copper, of which are made

rings, pendants, and other toys for the savages. [Webster]

care a continental

"I don't *care a continental*," i.e. [I don't care] at all. Central Connecticut. [Mead]

car-house

A garage. Texas. [Atwood]

carry

Escort. "Shall you *carry* Miss Smith to the picnic?" Louisiana. [Pearce]

car toad

On a railroad, the car inspector and similar workers who are concerned with the examination of wheels and bearings while a train is at a station or in the yard; in carnival and circus circles, the mechanic who looks after minor repairs on the cars. The work requires the men to stoop or squat by the side of the rolling stock in which position their likeness to a toad is not hard to see. [Irwin]

catalog woman

A wife secured through a matrimonial bureau. West. [R. Adams]

catch crop

A crop which, under favourable climatic conditions, is obtained from land intended for fallow, from seed . . . of a previous year's crop. Western Canada. [Sandilands]

catish

Stylish, elegant; generally preceded by *very*. Cincinnati. [Hart]

cat's light

The dusk or twilight; or in the language of the Scottish poet, "between the gloamin' and the mirk." Western Canada. [Sandilands]

cat wagon

Until the enactment of the "white slave" law of 1913, prostitution was carried on in some degree in rural communities by means of traveling wagons, usually covered and drawn by horses. Kansas. [Ruppenthal] *Cat's nest,* a house of ill repute. Western Indiana. [Brown]

cavallard

A term used in Louisiana and Texas by the caravans which cross the prairies to denote a band of horses or mules; [from] Spanish *caballada.* [Bartlett] *Cavvies,* stray cattle of which the owners are unknown, taken along and returned to their proper range. Wyoming. [Bruner]

cawhalux

The noise made by a box on the ear. [Bartlett]

cellar-smeller

A young man who always turns up where liquor is to be had without cost. Bryn Mawr College. [Savage]

chair barnacle

A bum who sits in railway depot waiting rooms, flophouse halls, and wherever else he may be tolerated. [Kane] *Depot-rounder,* an habitual lounger at a railway station. Northwestern Arkansas. [Carr] *Library bird,* a tramp who frequents libraries in order to avoid bad weather. [Irwin]

chair post

The leg of a chair. [Thornton]

change your breath

An injunction to adopt a different manner or bearing. An offensive slang expression which, originating in California, quickly ran its course through the Union. [Farmer & Henley]

chase

To recline in a chair in the sunshine; [recorded in] Colorado sanitoriums. [Harvey]

checkerboard crew

A gang containing both white and negro workers or convicts. [Weseen]

chemiloon

The chemise and drawers united in one garment. [Farmer]

chestnut-bell

A small bell worn on the shirt or waistcoat of a dandy and covered by the coat. The bell, activated by a spring, was rung whenever a worn-out story [a "chestnut"] was told. Snake County, Missouri. [Taylor]

chew one's tobacco twice

To repeat a remark. Arkansas. [Hanford]

chicken-flutter

Undue excitement, as "He's a *chicken-flutter.*" Cape Cod. [Chase]

chimbly corner laws

Customs that have been transmitted from generation to generation until they finally assume the nature of unwritten laws. The same term applies to unprofessional and usually erroneous interpretations of the statutes. Snake County, Missouri. [Taylor]

chinchy

Infested with bed-bugs; from *chinch,* a bed-bug. Eastern Alabama. [Payne]

chinkerings

Feminine sickness. Central Pennsylvania. [Shoemaker]

chips and grindstones

Odds and ends, general merchandise. A workman who is

paid in *chips and grindstones* gets no cash, but is forced to accept feed, groceries, dry goods and the like. [Randolph & Wilson]

chipwagon

A two-wheeled wagon for gathering "cow chips." West. [Berrey]

chirk

In a comfortable state; cheerful. . . . It should be remarked that the adjective *chirk* is used only in the interior of New England, and even there only by the illiterate. It is never heard in seaport towns. [Pickering]

chopping bee

In the old pioneer days, a new settler would frequently receive neighborly assistance in operations which, unaided, would would be out of his power to carry through in anything like reasonable time. A chopping-bee is thus described in *Western Magazine*: "The inhabitants within a radius of ten miles were invited. Each one brought his axe and day's provisions. . . . The front ranks of trees, ten rods in width, were chopped partially through on either side; then the succeeding ones in like manner for a space of perhaps twenty rods. . . . And thus for three days did this volunteer war against the forest progress." . . . *Stoning-bee,* a party of neighbors and friends who meet to clear a newcomer's plot of stones. [Farmer] *Beefing-bee,* an assembly of people for the purpose of slaughtering cattle. [Clapin] *Dry bee,* a bee at which no liquor was served. Canada. [Scargill]

chuck-a-tuck

Full. Newfoundland. [England]

chuck of a gal

A medium-size girl. North Carolina. [Cooper]

churchmaul

To discipline ecclesiastically. [Tucker]

cider oil

Cider concentrated by boiling, to which honey is subsequently added. Also called *cider royal*—probably the original name—such being found in old receipt books. [Bartlett]

Cincinnati oysters

Pigs' trotters. A curious interchange of names seems, not infrequently, to occur between fish, flesh, and fowl. In *Cincinnati oysters* we have flesh presented in the guise of fish, and the reverse is the case when the sturgeon is spoken of as *Albany beef*. Amongst other examples may be quoted *Marblehead turkey* for a codfish. Nor is the practice confined to America. In English slang, a *Billingsgate pheasant* is a fresh herring, whilst a *Yarmouth bloater* is sometimes called a "two-eyed steak." Indeed, many examples might be given of this strange perversion of terms. [Farmer]

circusing

Playing circus. "The boys played circus for three days . . . and then *circusing* was abandoned." —Mark Twain's *Tom Sawyer*. [Ramsay]

citizen rifle

The muzzle-loading Kentucky rifle. Probably so called to distinguish it from military weapons. Ozarks. [Randolph]

clam-butcher

A man who opens clams; the attendant at an oyster-bar is an *oyster-butcher*. [Farmer & Henley]

clam-digger's hands

As cold as a clam-digger's hands is about as cold as you can get, unless you add "in January." . . . Another occupational simile used by Mainers in the same way is "cold as a well-digger's elbows." [Gould]

clatchy

Cluttered. "This room is as *clatchy* as a second-hand store." Nebraska. [Pound]

clatterwhacking

A clatter, racket. [Bartlett]

clean as a hound's tooth

Very clean. New York. [Hanford]

clean shirt in a dog-fight

"As long as a *clean shirt in a dog-fight*," a short time. Northwest Arkansas. [Carr]

clear grit

Clear grit is that sterling manhood and womanhood that is always true to its own nature, and therefore in some sense to that highest nature in whose image we are made, no matter what may befall. As a diamond is a diamond all the same, you know whether it blazes on the brow of an emperor or is hid under the mountain peaks. [Schele de Vere]

clip and clean

Completely, entirely. "He missed me *clip and clean*." Maine, West Virginia. [Wentworth]

clip in

To run in for a short visit, as "I think I'll *clip in* to Mary's on the way home." It implies a hurried call, and if the visitor announces that he just clipped in, he is not expected to tarry for more than a few minutes. Nantucket. [Macy]

clitchy

Clammy, sticky. [Pickering]

clockify

There is a tendency to coin verbs ending in *fy* and *ify: ar-*

gufy instead of argue, *speechify* instead of orate, and so on. One [Ozark man] boasted that he could *clockify,* meaning that he knew how to repair clocks. [Randolph]

close to one's belly

To live *close to one's belly,* to live a hand-to-mouth existence. [Kane]

cloudesley-shovel

An awkward or lethargic person. "Wake up, you big *cloudsley-shovel.*" Nebraska. [Pound]

coach-abower

The sound of an invisible coach and horses on a gravel road, usually considered an omen of death. Central Pennsylvania. [Shoemaker]

coach-abower

cockarouse

A title of honor among the Indians of Virginia, and long afterwards used by the English settlers as a term for a person of consequence. "A *cockarouse* is one that has the honor to be of the king or queen's council, with relation to the affairs of government." —Robert Beverley's

The History and Present State of Virginia, 1705. [Bartlett]

codfish aristocracy

An opprobrious name for persons who have made money in [the fishing] trade. [Thornton]

coffee-pot sailor

A term used at the beginning of the twentieth century to indicate a sailor who had transferred from a sailing vessel to steam. The early steamships were called "kettle-bottomed coffee pots" by the sailing fraternity. [Tallman]

coffin tack

A cigarette. Pacific Northwest. [Harvey]

cohees

[A nickname] applied to the people of certain settlements in Western Pennsylvania from their use of the archaic form, "Quo' he"—he said. [Lowell]

cohogle

To bamboozle. Kentucky. [Dunglison]

cohonc

A year; so called from wild geese which, in their flight during their annual migrations, constantly utter a cry resembling *cohonc*. It was natural for people living in a state of nature in the depths of boundless forests, whose observations were bounded, to lay a stress on such a natural circumstance as attracted their attention. The animals themselves, by natural onomatopœia, were also called *honc*. [Boucher]

cohosses

[In the Connecticut River's] northern parts are three great bendings called *cohosses*, about one hundred miles asunder. [Peters]

coin notes

Notes payable in coin. [Thornton]

cold bread

The adjective *cold* is constantly applied to bread that is not cold at all, but simply not hot; also to stale bread. [Bartlett]

cold jaw

A horse that does not respond to bridal signals. [Weseen]

college farmer

Derogatory term for a farmer who has attended an agricultural college but has little practical experience. Canada. [Scargill]

colluvies

A collection of filth; excrement. The fluid mass into which the earth was supposed to be dissolved by the [biblical] Deluge; from Latin. [Worcester]

colt-man

A man who keeps horses specially for burglars. [Barrère]

Columbia leprosy

A euphemism for some disease, probably syphilis. Canada. [Scargill]

comb the head

The expression is always *comb the head,* never the hair. Southern Illinois. [Rice]

comeatable

Capable of being approached or "come at." Virginia. [Green]

come-outers

Come-outers is not only the name of a religious sect, numerous in New England, but a cant term for all who are said to have *come out* from some organized society. [Schele de Vere] They hold a diversity of opinions on many points, some believing in the divine inspiration of the Scriptures, and others that they are but human compositions. [Bartlett]

come-up-with

To get one's *come-up-with* means to meet with one's deserts, more or less unpleasantly. A New England expression. [Thornton]

common doings

Fat pork. "Corn bread and *common doings*," bread made of Indian meal and fat pork in the Far West. [Marryat]

common plugs

The common rut of mankind; the *hoi polloi*, sometimes the "great unwashed," but more commonly very ordinary people indeed—neither the big-wigs nor the dregs of society. [Barrère]

company bread

Bread carried to keep off fairies. Newfoundland. [England]

composuist

A writer, composer. This extraordinary word has been much used at some of our colleges, but very seldom elsewhere. . . . A correspondent observes that it is used in England among musicians. [Pickering]

compushency

Compulsion; necessity. Kansas. [Ruppenthal]

conkerbill

An icicle. Newfoundland. [England]

consociation

This term, which signifies, as Mr. Webster explains it, "a convention of pastors and messengers of churches," is used in Connecticut. [Pickering]

continenent, the

The islander's name for the mainland of North America. Nantucket. [Macy]

coof

An "off-islander." Said to have been applied originally only to Cape Codders. Nantucket. [Macy]

cooling-board

The board on which a dead body is laid out. Pennsylvania and Maryland. [Bartlett]

coon-footed

Having toes turned out. Virginia. [Dingus]

corned

When a man is tipsy, they generally say he is *corned*, spirits being made from corn. [Marryat]

cornfield clemo

An escape from prison by sneaking away from a work gang; [from] *clemo*, executive clemency in the form of a commutation or a parole. [Weseen]

corn-right

In early times, a right acquired by settlers who, by planting an acre or more of corn, were entitled to one hundred acres of land. Virginia. [Bartlett]

corn-stealer

The hand. "I shall have the exquisite pleasure of shaking your *corn-stealer*." North Carolina. [Eliason] *Cornstealers*, the hands. [Farmer & Henley]

corporosity

The human body; a Pennsylvania idiom. [Farmer]

cotbetty

An American compound of the English *cot*—which English glossaries quote as meaning an effeminate, troublesome man—and the term *betty*, used very much in the same sense, is occasionally heard to denote a man who meddles with a woman's special duties in a household. [Schele de Vere]

cottagely

Rustic; suitable to a cottage. [Whitney]

couch-ache

"Fred gave Fran and I so many sour plumbs that we both had the *couch-ache*." North Carolina. [Eliason]

counter-hopper

A cad. "This town is full of *counter-hoppers* that go around and tell every girl they meet that they are moving picture actors." Montana. [Hayden]

count the ties

To walk the railroad tracks when one hasn't the money to ride. Eastern Alabama. [Payne]

Cousin Jennie

A Cornishwoman. Companion to the universal *Cousin Jack* for a Cornishman. Coeur d'Alene, Idaho. [Lehman] *Cousin Jack,* a Welsh miner; *Cousin Anne,* a Welsh miner's wife; *Cousin Michael,* a German. [Berrey]

cover with the moon

To sleep in the open. [Irwin]

cow college

Agricultural college; of the University of Minnesota. [Klaeber]

cow's breakfast

A hat, especially a straw hat. Canada. [Scargill] *Mule's breakfast,* a straw mattress or bed. [Berrey]

cranberry-eye

A bloodshot eye. [Farmer & Henley]

crawfish

The English term *to rat,* as applied to members who suddenly back out from a position they have long maintained, is in America replaced by the equally suggestive term to *crawfish* or *crayfish,* derived from the peculiar locomotion of the animal. The use of the word originated in the West but has become quite general. [Schele de Vere] To back out. "We made a fair trade, but he *crawfished*." Southeastern Missouri. [Crumb]

Cream City

Milwaukee, from the cream-colored bricks from which its houses are built. [Johnson]

crimpy weather

Bad weather; [from] *crimps,* rheumatism. [Kane]

crooked stick

A man who has turned out to be a failure in life. No dishonesty of character is implied. Southwestern Wisconsin. [Savage]

cross-roader

A man whose ways are doubtful or dishonest. [Barrère]

crowd the mourners

To be in a hurry. Used only in the expression "don't *crowd the mourners.*" Western Indiana. [Brown]

crust coffee

A beverage made by boiling burnt or scorched crusts. Canada. [Scargill] In our early history, when transportation costs made coffee very expensive, various substitutes were attempted. Potatoes were . . . roasted or burned, [and] ground in a mill or reduced to a powder in a mortar. A like method was used on parched rye, chestnuts, and dandelion roots. [Tallman]

Cupid's itch

Any venereal disease. [Irwin]

curb-stone brokers

Stock operators whose place of business is on the edge of the pavement in the vicinity of the Merchants' Exchange [New York] and whose account-books are said to be kept in their hats. A more recent name for curb-stone breakers is *gutter-snipes*. [Bartlett]

curl one's liver

To experience intensity of feeling—enjoyable or otherwise. "[Steamboat-racing] makes a body's very liver curl with enjoyment." —Mark Twain's *Life on the Mississippi*. [Farmer]

curwhibbles

Unsteady or fantastic motions of man or beast, such as those caused by too many glasses [of spirits]. "He was cuttin' the *curwibbles,* alright." Newfoundland. [Devine]

cut eyes

To meet someone's gaze and look away quickly. [Thornton]

cut money

Segments of coins circulating as units of value. "A considerable proportion of the little specie to be seen is what is called *cut money*—dollars cut into two, four, eight and sixteen pieces." —Timothy Flint's *Letters from America,* 1818. [Craigie]

cut no ice

That cuts no ice [is] equivalent to "is of no consequence," [or] "makes no difference." [Thornton]

cut up copper

To destroy a still. "Last winter there come a revenue [agent] in here and *cut up* a lot of *copper.*" North Carolina. [Kephart]

cut your foot

When a well-bred country boy is walking with his girl and sees that she is about to step into some cow dung, he says, "Don't *cut your foot*!" This euphemism is known to everybody in the backwoods and is sometimes used figuratively even in the pulpit. Ozarks. [Randolph & Wilson]

You may have a pretty considerable damned good sort of a fee-ble notion that it don't fit nohow; and that it ain't calculated to make you smart overmuch; and that you don't feel special bright, and by no means first-rate, and not at all tongue-y; and that however rowdy you may be by natur', it does use you up com-plete, and that's a fact; and makes you quake consider-able and disposed to damn the engine—all which phrases, I beg to add, are pure Americanisms of the first water.

—Letter mocking American English from Charles Dickens to
John Forster, dated February 24, 1842

daddock

Daddock, an old English term rarely heard abroad even in provincial dialects, is quite common in the rural districts of the New England states and not [infrequently] in the West, where the great long trunks of fallen trees, slowly rotting away and turning into mould, are thus called. [Schele de Vere]

danced in the pig trough

Remained single after an older brother or sister had mar-ried. North Carolina. [Cooper]

dance joober

To make a child *dance joober* is to whip him. Kentucky. [Fruit]

darsn't

Dares not; probably a negro corruption, and of Southern origin. Popular colloquially. [Farmer]

dawnies

In previous years, many people used *dawnies* to mean a nightmare. It suggests that the person is between consciousness and unconsciousness, a sort of dream. [To] *have the dawnies,* to be harried or tired; to be hung-over. Newfoundland. [Story]

dayshine

Daylight. [Lyons]

deacons' hiding-places

Curtained stalls in Boston oyster saloons. [Bartlett]

deadfall

Trees downed by wind, disease, or age. Canada. [Scargill]

dead in the shell

Utterly worn out. "If I have to go without sleep I'll be just *dead in the shell*." Kansas. [Ruppenthal]

dead-wool

Wool taken from the skins of sheep which . . . have died. [Whitney]

death on

Exceedingly fond of, or addicted to. [Thornton]

debtor's veil

Take the debtor's veil, to go into voluntary bankruptcy. [Weseen]

deceive one's looks

To be better or worse than one appears. Often used by

horse-traders in speaking of broken down steeds. Southeastern Missouri. [Crumb]

deceive one's looks

declaration-men

Those who signed the *Declaration of Independence.*
[Thornton]

dedodgement

Exit. Kentucky. [Dunglison]

dehorn

Anything which tends to ameliorate the condition of the
down-trodden working man such as shorter hours, better
housing conditions, etc., making him forget the oppres-
sion of capital, is regarded as *dehorn*. All kindness is regarded as propaganda which is cutting off the horns of the
worker. [Kane]

devil's birthday

The day on which pea soup is served. It was quite common for people to say, when pea soup was being served,
"It's the *devil's birthday* again." Newfoundland. [Story]

dew claws

The new growth of claws of an animal which is supposed

to shed its claws periodically. They are supposed to be particularly sharp. The term is used figuratively with reference to persons, as "That hill is so steep you have to stick your *dew claws* in to get up it." Aroostook, Maine. [Carr]

dictionatical

Such as the dictionary authorizes or approves. "I don't think that word is *dictionatical*." Kansas. [Ruppenthal]

diddle can

A bottle of whiskey; especially a container of bootleg whiskey. During Boonville's local-option "dry" era immediately after 1906, several bootleg operations flourished. A Dr. Diddle allegedly dispensed homemade spirits as "medicine." [*Diddle can* is a] combination of his name and *can,* a container. Boontling language. [C. Adams]

didoes

To cut up didoes, to play mischief. [Thornton]

die in the harness

To work until the end of life. [Weseen]

dight

A small portion, dab; as a *dight* of butter. Portsmouth, New Hampshire. [Allen] "I don't care a *dite,*" not at all or not a little bit. A New England survival from *doit.* [Farmer]

dig up the hatchet

To recall the cause of strife or renew the quarrel. Resume hostilities; break a peace agreed to by "burying the hatchet." Canada. [Scargill] *Dig up the tomahawk,* to declare war, to start trouble. [Weseen] *Dig up dead cats,* "Don't *dig up dead cats,*" don't recall disagreeable subjects. North Carolina. [Cooper]

dimension stuff

Dimension[-sawn] lumber. Kansas. [Ruppenthal]

dime of, nickel of

A dime's [or nickel's] worth. "A *dime of* bread." Louisiana. [Routh]

dinetical

Whirling round. [Webster]

dipe

"To go on the *dipe*," to pick pockets. The pickpocket himself is called a *dip*. "I felt very rough and was thinking I would have to go on the *dipe* again." —Mark Twain's *Life on the Mississippi*. [Farmer]

direful

Ridiculous; I have often heard an old eccentric fellow— lazy, funny, and sociable—called a *direful child*. Rhode Island. [Ellis]

disablest

Antonym of *ablest*. "Johnson's the *disablest* one of the family." North Carolina. [Kephart]

disrespectable

For disreputable. Dispite its seeming orthodoxy, an entirely spurious word. [Farmer]

diving-hooks

Appliances for picking pockets. [Thornton]

diz

To make dizzy; daze. "When that block fell on his head it *dizzed* him." Kansas. [Ruppenthal]

do brown

In Yankee terminology, if you were able to take advantage of someone, you had *done them brown*. [Tallman]

docious

A corruption of *docile*, as a *docious* young man. [Bartlett]

dockwalloper

A loiterer around docks. New York. [Tucker]

---

doctor-drummer

A solicitor of practice for a physician. "The government is going to do away with the *doctor-drummers* at hot springs." Northwestern Arkansas. [Carr]

doctor's trade

Drugs or medicines. New England. [Dunglison]

doctor medicine

Differentiated from home remedies. North Carolina. [Kephart]

do don't

A negroism, but generally colloquial in the South for *don't*. [Farmer]

doeface

In allusion to the female deer, which is frightened at her own shadow. Rhode Island. [Ellis]

doflickety

Any small article. Kansas. [Ruppenthal] *Majig,* short for *thingamajig.* [Atkinson] *Optriculum,* about the same as *doodad, thingumbob,* etc. Referring to a dish towel, "Where is that *optriculum*?" Nebraska. [Pound] *Dingclinker,* an unusually fine or pleasing person or thing. Maine, northern New Hampshire. [England]

dofunny

Any effective or labor-saving contrivance, particularly if novel. Southern Illinois. [Rice]

dogpelter

An imaginary official; used as a term of contempt in southeastern Missouri and southern Illinois. [Ramsay]

dog's foot

"The *dog's foot*! I'll do no such thing." Eastern Alabama. [Payne]

dogswawsted

Exclamation [of] exasperation, annoyance, or surprise. "I'll be *dogswawsted*!" Nebraska. [Pound]

dollar house

An inn or rest house at which any meal costs a dollar. . . . [The meal] generally consisted of beans and fat bacon, with bread or biscuit, and very thick coffee. Canada. [Scargill]

dollar native

An Eskimo of the Mackenzie Delta region who demands high pay for his services. [Scargill]

Don't hurry, Hopkins

Used ironically in the West in speaking to persons who are very slow in their work or tardy in meeting an obligation. It is said to have originated from the case of one Hopkins, who, having given one of his creditors a promissory note in regular form, added to it this extraordinary memorandum: "It is expressly agreed that the said Hopkins is not to be hurried in paying the above note." [Farmer]

doobobbus

Vague designation used when the exact word is not recalled or is purposely avoided. "Hasn't she a cute *doobobbus* on her head?" Nebraska. [Pound]

dooryard visit

Although still used with automobiles, this meant a buggy visit when the occupants didn't descend to come into the house. Maine. [Gould]

doozandazzy

Something, the name of which cannot be readily recalled. "Hand me that *doozandazzy*." *Mr., Mrs.* or *Miss Doozanberry*, in occasional use for one whose name is not known. Nebraska, Massachusetts, Kansas. [Pound]

double clock

To deceive or betray by double-dealing; to deceive in love, "two-time." *Double clocker,* one who fails to keep a promise. [Berrey]

double cousins

When two brothers marry two sisters, the children are known as *double cousins.* Such relationships are very common in the Ozarks, and are considered somehow significant. In referring to each other these people seldom say simply, "He's my cousin," but rather, "We're *double cousins.*" [Randolph & Wilson]

double horse

Doing double horse is doing, or being, two things at a time. [Farmer]

double in brass

To play in the band in addition to performing. Circus slang. [Weseen]

double O

To examine; to spy . . . *Single O,* a vagrant who travels alone; a criminal who works alone. [Weseen]

double-up

To marry. New Jersey. [Lee]

down cellar

Down cellar, for *down in,* or *into,* the cellar, is a common New England expression. So too is "up garret." [Bartlett]

Down East

Down East, in the American's mind, is instinctively placed near the low coast of the Atlantic, as if it were *down* toward the sea, and at the same time toward the east. The emigrant who has gone to the West still remembers with delight how they did *Down East,* and looks forward, after years of hard labor and painful longings, to visit the East, while the Virginian, to the second or third genereation even, speaks of . . . *coming in*, when he proposes to visit his relatives in the Old Dominion. The *Down Easter* is well known by his language, his costume, and his peculiar habits, smiled at for many an odd trick he has, but respected for his many odd virtues. With him, all that is done in his native land is right, and hence what he admires he simply calls *about East*. [Schele de Vere]

down-go

Decline in health. "I love strong coffee, but when I get on the *down-go* I cain't hardly drink it." North Carolina, Kentucky. [Kephart]

down in the bushes

Sick; in hard luck. Used in the mountains of Oregon. [Harvey]

down on his uppers

To be in poor circumstances. . . . The "upper is" the part of the shoe above the sole, so a man who is *down on his uppers* is scuffing along with his bare feet practically on the ground, without money to get his shoes tapped. New England. [Haywood] *On his uppers,* to be without money. New Mexico. [Warnock]

down-scent

A downward slope, declivity, or descent; downhill. A blend of *descent* and *downhill.* Newfoundland. [Story]

down to the ground

An American rendering of the word *entirely,* as "That suits me *down to the ground.*" [Hotten]

dreaming stage

A tree platform used by Indians to commune with their special spirits during the ritual marking the progress from puberty to manhood. Canada. [Scargill]

dressed like a sore finger

Overdressed. New Mexico. [Warnock]

dress into numbers

To don a prison uniform. [Weseen]

driet

Drying power in the weather prevailing. "There's no *driet* in the weather." Newfoundland. [Devine]

drive home the beef

To win everything at stake. The figure is from the shooting match in which one or more beeves were the prizes. The most expert shot won the four quarters and the hide, and therefore could drive his beef home ["on the hoof"]. Southwestern Wisconsin. [Savage]

driving the nail

Among the favorite amusements of Western men are naturally trials of skill with their rifles. At one time they will bet on *driving the nail*. A stout nail is driven into a post about half-way up to the head. The riflemen then stand at a great distance and fire at the nail, the object being to hit the nail so truly on the head with the ball as to drive it home. [Schele de Vere]

dropgate

A passageway made by holding down the wires of a fence. Kansas. [Ruppenthal]

drop one's candy

To make a big blunder; to do something to cause the failure of a plan. Probably the phrase originated at the candy-pullings, which were often held out of doors. If one "dropped his candy," he naturally lost it on account of the grit and dirt. Eastern Alabama. [Payne]

drozzle

A slovenly woman. [Thornton]

dry drizzle

A light shower of rain. Snake County, Missouri. [Taylor]

dry grins

To have the dry grins, said of one sorely teased but striving to smile. Virginia. [Dingus] *Dry gripes*, a revulsion of feelings; a strong repugnance. [Ramsay]

dry so

Plainly; just so. "I told him *dry so* I didn't believe him." Southern Missouri. [Crumb]

dry wilts

A condition of extreme decrepitude or desiccation. "That old feller's got the *dry wilts*, an' he looks plumb foolish a-runnin' after them gals." Ozarks. [Randolph & Wilson] A person who looks seedy from illness or other cause is referred to as looking as though he was "struck with the dry wilt." Nantucket. [Macy]

duck's quack

Excellent; desirable. The *cat's whiskers*, attractive, desirable, splendid. . . . Variant expressions used in the same way are the cat's *eyebrow, ankle, adenoids, tonsils, pajamas, galoshes, cufflinks, roller skates,* and *cradle.* [Weseen]

ducy

The penis; pronounced so as to rhyme with *Lucy.* The word seems to be used mostly by the old women in the Ozarks. [Randolph]

dudess

A female dude. [Mathews] *Dudette, dudinette,* a very young girl; a mere chit who affects the airs and style of a belle. [Barrère] *Dudine* and *dudene* are variants. *Dudelet,* a child of eastern tourists vacationing on a ranch. [Weseen] *Dudelette,* a mentally and physically stunted male of any age, to whom dress—and frequently overdressing—is the Alpha and Omega of life. . . . One generally finds such dressy individuals do not, as a rule, patronize the best custom tailors, but rather purchase garments of ephemeral style. Western Canada. [Sandilands]

dull as a frow

Very dull; said of any cutting tool. The name *frow* [a wedge for splitting shingles, lath, or barrel staves] is almost entirely lost sight of, but the expression is a common one. Eastern Alabama. [Payne]

dumb-betty

A washing machine. [Farmer] Barrel-shaped, with a rotary shank. [Bartlett] A name applied to a mechanical contrivance serving some household function. "Jefferson's *dumb betty*, without the attendance of a servant, serves up his chocolate and hot muffins for breakfast." —*Massachusetts Spy*, May 14, 1814. [Craigie]

Dutch-cheese

Cottage cheese. Western New York. [Bowen]

Dutch crossing

A crossing of a street in the middle of a block. Louisiana. [Routh]

Dutchman

A German. [Thornton]

Dutchman's breeches

A small patch of blue sky at the end of a storm. [Colcord]

The words continually used among the people are, in num-
berless cases, not the words used in writing or recorded in the
dictionaries by authority. There are just as many words in
daily use not inscribed in the dictionary, and seldom or never
in any print. . . . The Real Dictionary will give all the words
that exist in use—the bad words as well as any. . . . The English language is grandly lawless, like the race who use[s] it—or
rather breaks out of the little laws to enter truly the higher
ones.

—American poet Walt Whitman's lecture *An American Primer*,
written in the early to mid-1850s and first published
posthumously in *The Atlantic Monthly* (April 1904)

ear-settin'

A scolding; a reprimand. An adaptation of the expression
"to set an ear," the lingo for *scold*. It is an allusion to the
method of punishing sheep dogs for misconduct by twist-
ing their ears. Boontling language. [C. Adams]

Easter before Lent

This was an expression used by the Creole folk of
Louisiana to indicate that a baby had been born too soon
after the wedding. [Tallman]

eat after

Used with reference to the preparation of food. "Thet ol' woman's th' best cook I ever *et after*." Ozarks. [Randolph]

eating tobacco

Chewing tobacco. Canada. [Scargill]

egg-harbor

A dance hall where no admission is charged. Bryn Mawr College. [Savage]

eighty-eight

"Love and kisses" in the lingo of the telegraph operator; sent as figures, *88*. *Seventy-three,* "best wishes" in the telegrapher's code; sent as figures, *73*. *Thirty,* telegrapher's name for the end of a shift—also for death. [Weseen]

elevenses

Neck muscles. "Oh, the poor man—his *elevenses* are up." This means a person is fading, not long for this world, because the two muscles in the back of the neck stick out like two bones, resembling *11*. Newfoundland. [Story]

elk-face

Physiognomy in which the cheek furrows run nearly parallel with the nose. Kansas. [Ruppenthal]

embowel

To enclose in something. [Lyons]

empt

From the participle *emptied,* a word coined by old ladies in New England, as "Go *empt* out the water." [Bartlett] It is an ungracious thing to deprive ladies, especially old ones, of the fruit of their mental labors, but there is hardly a house in some quarters of [New] England where this old provincialism is not still current. [Farmer]

end of creation

A person or thing of extremely little consequence. Kansas.
[Ruppenthal]

end of steel

Just that point in a new country to which railway construction has advanced. *End of steel* thus appears in the
list of post offices, and assumes the importance of a village or town. Western Canada. [Sandilands] *End-of-
steel town,* a community at the end of a railway line.
[Scargill]

English basement

A basement on the level of the ground, or approximately
so; a high basement. [Craigie]

Englishment

Something anglicized. [Farmer]

English milk

In Indian parlance, rum. Canada. "The Indians were anx-
iously awaiting me, to taste the 'new milk,' as they generally call rum." —Elliott Coues's *New Light on the Early
History of the Greater Northwest,* 1803. [Scargill]

ensmall

To condense. A facetious word modeled on *enlarge.*
[Farmer]

eternal camping ground

A simile for a future state of existence, borrowed from the
phraseology of backwoodsmen. [Farmer]

eujifferous

Grand; fine; splendid. "I had a perfectly *eujifferous* time."
Nebraska. [Pound]

Excellency

This title is, in America, given by courtesy to governors of
states. [Farmer]

excited as a cat at a mouse-show

Highly excited. Maine, northern New Hampshire. [England]

exflunct

Demolish. [Tucker] To overcome or beat thoroughly. To "use up" completely. Also, *exfluncticate, exflunctify.* [Craigie]

extermish

A combination of *exterminate* and *abolish.* Northeastern Ohio. [Wentworth]

There is no basis for the belief that somewhere there exists a sublimated English language, perfect and impeccable. This is the flawless ideal to which all artists in style strive vainly to attain, whether they are Englishmen or Americans, Australians or Canadians, Irish or Scotch. But nowhere is this speech without stain spoken by man in his daily life—not in London, where cockneyisms abound, not in Oxford, where university slang is luxuriant and where pedantry flourishes. Nowhere has this pure and undefiled language ever been spoken by any community. Nowhere will it ever be spoken, other than by a few men here and there gifted by nature or trained by art.

—American author James Brander Matthews's
Americanisms and Briticisms (1892)

fairlick

At Harvard University, a football term used when the ball is fairly caught or kicked beyond bounds. [Barrère]

fair off

A Southern term denoting that the weather is clearing up slowly. [Schele de Vere]

false pond

A mirage. "The most perplexing phenomenon, occasioned

by optical illusion, is the mirage, or as familiarly called on the prairies, the *false ponds*." —Josiah Gregg's *Commerce of the Prairies*, 1844. [Craigie]

farziner

A vulgar contraction of *far-as-I-know,* extensively used through New England and New York, including Long Island. [Bartlett]

fate and dumplings

"In spite of *fate and dumplings*," at any cost. "He vowed he'd finish the job in spite of *fate and dumplings*." Southwestern Wisconsin. [Savage]

favor

Resemble. "She *favors* her father more than her mother." Southeastern Missouri. [Crumb]

feather-legged

Cowardly. North Carolina. [Cooper]

feel pale

To *feel pale* is a humorous way of saying one is sick. [Bartlett]

feels his corn

Of a frisky fat horse we say he *feels his corn*. Kentucky. [Fruit]

fence-corner peach

Any good-looking country girl may be called a *fence-corner peach,* but the term often implies a low-class family background or questionable paternity. I asked an old friend about this and he answered, "Well, the trees in the fence-corners was all seedlin's, you know. Just growed up accidental, not planted in no regular orchard. But they was the best peaches I ever tasted." Ozarks. [Randolph & Wilson]

fence-jumpin'

Adultery; acts of marital infidelity. An allusion to one's

leaving his own pasture to graze somewhere else. Boontling language. [C. Adams]

fetch up

To stop suddenly. The sense of the word is not noticed in the English dictionaries nor by Webster. "He *fetched up* all standing," that is, he made a sudden halt. The more common phrase with us is, "He *brought up* all standing." It is a nautical vulgarism, the figure being that of a ship which is suddenly brought to while at full speed and with her sails set. [Bartlett]

fiddle-faced

Sorrowful; sad; gloomy. [Weseen]

fiddle-faced

fifth calf

Anything supernumerary; same as *fifth wheel*. New England. [Hanford]

fill one's shirt

To eat heartily. Southwestern Wisconsin. [Savage]

fine as frog-hair

Extra fine. Arkansas. [Hanford]

fip, levy

The Spanish silver coins which were long current in

some parts of the Union have nearly all disappeared and with them their local names, as *fip* and *levy,* coins representing six and a quarter and twelve and a half cents. The former [was] a contraction of "five pence," through the English *fippence,* the latter the scant remnant of *eleven pence.* "A fip's worth of dinner and a levy's worth of sleep" were the words of a loafer of Philadelphia, where the names remained longest in use. [Schele de Vere] *Levy,* elevenpence. . . . Sometimes called an *eleven-penny bit.* [Bartlett]

fire-new

New from the forge; brand-new. This old and nearly obsolete expression is sometimes used by us. "You should have accosted her; and with some excellent jests, *fire-new* from the mint, you should have banged the youth into darkness." —Shakespeare's *Twelfth Night.* [Bartlett]

first hop

At the first hop, immediately. [Thornton]

first lunch

A woodsman's early breakfast, eaten at 5:00 a.m. *Second lunch,* a woodsman's second breakfast, eaten at 9:00 a.m. *Third lunch,* a woodsman's third meal of the day, eaten at 1:00 p.m. Eastern Maine. [Carr]

First of May

A novice; a person out for his first season. Circus and carnival slang. [Weseen]

fishing for love

Not catching any fish. "Have any luck? No, I'm *fishing for love.*" Northwest Arkansas. [Carr]

fish-proud

Self-satisfied because of a large catch of cod. Newfoundland. [Story]

fisticate

Proceeding from *fisticuff,* meaning to quarrel, to meddle, to fight. We read in Capt. John Smith's *Account of Virginia,* "There are so many *fisticating* tobacco-mungers in England." [Clapin]

five-center

Probably formed on the analogy of *five-dollar.* "Jim always kept that *five-center* piece 'round his neck with a string." —Mark Twain's *Huckleberry Finn.* [Ramsay]

five-finger

A thief. [Weseen] *Ten fingers,* oysterman's slang for *thief;* not very common. New Jersey. [Lee]

five to four

Not unanimous; hence open to question as to its correctness or justice. In allusion to several important decisions of the U.S. Supreme Court wherein the justices stood five and four. . . . It is widely used by press and bar far beyond Kansas. [Ruppenthal]

fix one's flint

To settle one's business. [Thornton]

flabberdegaz

Vain imaginings in speech. Pacific Northwest. [Lehman]

flambustious

Gaudy; showy. [Weseen]

flat road

In logging, a forest path chopped so that flood water may carry rafts through. Louisiana. [Rontt]

flat side of earth

This side of the grave. "The schoolmaster hain't got a friend on the *flat side of earth.*" [Farmer]

fleeper

A petty informer. [Goldin]

flimp

To wrestle; to tustle. [Weseen]

flip-floppussed

Played out; in a state of collapse. A variation of the American usage of *to flummox* and *to flop*. Said to be common in Arkansas. [Farmer]

flippercanorious

Fine; grand. "I feel *flippercanorious* today." Nebraska. [Pound]

flipper dinner

A traditional meal of seal flippers. Newfoundland. [Scargill]

flitflats

To give one the flitflats, to make one nervous. Kansas. [Ruppenthal]

floodwood

Driftwood. [Tucker]

flookum

A powder containing flavoring and coloring for soft drinks. Circus and carnival slang. [Weseen]

flopshion

Agitation; "all of a *flopshion*," flustered. Newfoundland. [England]

flugins

A word used to some extent by all classes, generally in the following connection: "It is as cold as *flugins*." I do not know either the origin or the exact meaning [but] it seems to be merely an intensive. Mississippi. [Shands]

flummadiddle

A few of the terms used on board ship may be regarded as belonging to our speech exclusively. Such is the *flummadiddle,* a holiday mess of New England fishermen, who lick their chops at the very mention of this oddly named delicacy. It consists of a number of ingredients, the most important of which are stale bread, pork-fat, molasses, cinnamon, allspice, and cloves. By the aid of these materials a kind of mush is made which is baked in the oven and brought to the table hot and brown. [Schele de Vere]

flying ginny

A merry-go-round. Originally the propelling power was furnished by a mule [or "ginny"]. Northwest Arkansas. [Carr] *Flying horses,* carousel or merry-go-round. New Orleans. [Riedel]

footy

A mistake; a simpleton; a blunderer; anyone slightly valued. Local in Massachusetts. [Bartlett] Small, insignificant. There is also a New England expression, "footin' around," fussing, busying oneself uselessly. [Lee]

Ford marriage

A union usually born of gasoline and good nature. The man and woman continue to live together, traveling about the country from job to job in a car until the man tires of his consort, or until she becomes pregnant and seems likely to become a burden, when she is deserted. If the two get along well together, or if the man is "easy," or has a sense of responsibility, a "Ford family" results. [Irwin]

foreparents

Forefathers. North Carolina, Tennessee, Arkansas. [Kephart]

forgettery

Facetious for memory, or poor memory. "I'll store that in my *forgettery.*" Nebraska. [Pound]

forty-jawed

Excessively talkative. Pacific Northwest. [Hayden]

forty-'leven

An almost ludicrous slang term, possibly of negro manufacture, is the expression *forty-'leven*. The first part is, in all probability, the familiar number used, like other round numbers in Hebrew, as an indefinite expression. Boys say, "You scare me like forty," and teamsters boast of a powerful horse that will "pull like forty." The addition of *eleven* is the element of incongruity added to the humorous exaggeration already expressed, and thus a *forty-'leventh* cousin, for instance, expresses an infinitesimal degree of relationship, one too small to be stated accurately. [Schele de Vere]

forty-miler

A term used by carnival folk of an enterprise that does not get more than forty miles from its home town. For bigger outfits on the move, a "small jump" was a trip up to a hundred miles, while a "big jump" was one of two to four hundred miles. [Tallman]

forty rows of apple trees

"Not within forty rows of apple trees," to be very far from. "That don't come within *forty rows of apple trees* of being the right size." Western New York. [Bowen]

fotch-on

Homemade; opposite to "store-bought." North Carolina. [Cooper] Not made or produced in the neighborhood. "I cain't stomach them *fotch-on* beans out 'n cans." Ozarks. [Randolph]

found

Fined; past tense of *fine*. "He was convicted and *found* five dollars." Southern Missouri. [Crumb]

found-in

A person arrested for being present in a brothel or an illegal drinking establishment. Canada. [Scargill]

found missing

To be *found missing,* in Western parlance, to be absent or to run away. [Schele de Vere]

fourbled, fivebled

I recollect once talking with one of the first men in America, who was narrating to me the advantages which might have accrued to him if he had followed up a certain speculation, when he said, "Sir, if I had done so, I should not only have doubled and trebled, but I should have *fourbled* and *fivebled* my money." [Marryat]

fourth-class liberty

Scanning the shore, especially with binoculars, when restricted aboard ship. [Bradford]

Fourth of July

A shutdown. The term comes from the practice of laying off for a period after the Fourth of July until enough men have sobered up to get the operation going again. Pacific Northwest. [McCulloch]

fracture-box

A box used to encase a fractured leg, securing immobility and facilitating the application of dressings. [Whitney]

fraggle

In Texas, people are not robbed—they are only *fraggled,* which amounts to much the same thing. [Farmer]

frateriority

An organization that admits both boys and girls. College slang. [Weseen]

frenchy

Light-headed, frivolous. "I don't like *frenchy* girls." Pacific Northwest. [Hayden]

fresh cat

A flannel cloth soaked, or "fried," in hot grease and hung

like an apron over the chest for protection and curative purposes in treatment of croup, colds, etc. Eastern Alabama. [Payne]

freshwater town, freshwater college

One speaks . . . of regions further inland with the qualifying adjective *freshwater,* as in *freshwater towns* or *freshwater colleges,* the adjective carrying with it some implication of rusticity or provincialism. [Krapp]

frost-smoke

A thick, black vapor arising in winter. Ontario. [Chamberlain]

fruice

A blend of *fruit* and *juice.* The name was used in the late nineties, and for some time thereafter, for a non-alcoholic punch or drink served at receptions, etc. especially by those interested in temperence reform. Nebraska. [Pound]

fruitist

A cultivator of fruit trees. One of a class of words [ending in] *ist,* some of which are useful but which in the main are hideous monstrosities. What in the world can be said for such forms as *walkist, shootist, singist, landscapist,* and (Oh Minerva!) *obituarist?* [Farmer]

full chisel

Strenuously; at full tilt. [Thornton] A metaphor from a chisel which, when not struck properly, starts off violently sidewise. . . . A modern New England vulgarism. [Bartlett] *Full butt,* with sudden collision. The figure is taken from the violent encounter of animals, such as rams or goats, which butt with their heads. [Bartlett]

fumadiddle

A western term for fancy dress. *Faradiddle* and *fofaraw* are also used in this sense. These unusual words have been

used in the West since the early trappers and scouts. . . .
Fofaraw is probably from *fanfaron,* meaning showy trifles, gaudy finery, and other gewgaws. West. [R. Adams]

funeral-card

The printed notice of death posted on a telegraph-pole or
some other convenient place. Peterboro, Ontario. [Cham-
berlain]

The coloni[e]s are composed of adventurers, not only from every district of Great Britain and Ireland but from almost every other European government, where the principles of liberty and commerce have operated with spirit and efficacy. Is it not therefore reasonable to suppose that the English language must be greatly corrupted by such a strange intermixture of various nations? The reverse is, however, true. The language of the intermediate descendants of such a promiscuous ancestry is perfectly uniform and unadulterated; nor has it borrowed any provincial or national accent from its British or foreign parentage.

—English visitor William Ellis, writing home in a letter dated June 8, 1770, published in 1792 in *Letters from America, Historical and Descriptive, 1769 to 1777*

gabble-tonguey

Loquacious. [Atkinson]

gal-boy

Gal-boy is in New England used occasionally for the more familiar *tom-boy*. [Schele de Vere] A girlish boy. [Bartlett]

galley-west

To *knock galley-west*, to bring to confusion; to knock out completely, dispose of finally. "Says enough to knock their little game *galley-west*, doesn't it?" —Mark Twain's *Life on the Mississippi*. [Ramsay] An odd sailor's expression, often heard, but the origin of which is obscure. . . . The *galley* doubtless refers to the cookhouse. But why *west* rather than east, or any other point of the compass? Nantucket. [Macy] *Sky west end crooked,* helpless; senseless. "He knocked him *sky west end crooked.*" Northwest Arkansas. [Carr]

galloping dominoes
The game of dice. [Weseen]

galvanize
Nickel plating. "The *galvanize* wore off my pistol." North Carolina. [Kephart]

galvanized Yankee
The poor Confederate soldier who succumbed morally to the privations and sufferings of the Northern prisons and penitentiaries, and in his dire need took the oath [of allegiance] and enlisted in the United States Army, was contemptuously called a *galvanized Yankee.* [Schele de Vere]

gapper's cut
A small percentage of loot given to one who has observed but not actively participated in [a robbery; from] *gapper,* one who gapes, especially a bystander who might hinder the execution of a crime. [Goldin]

Garden of America
Long Island is called the Garden of America. [Fearon]

gawnmoge
To deceive. [Story] *Gomogues,* clownish tricks and play. Newfoundland. [Devine]

gay quaker
A quaker dressing less soberly than others. [Thornton]

gehuncled
Crippled. [Weseen]

gentleman turkey

The mock modesty of the Western states requires that a male turkey should be so called. [Bartlett] *He-biddy,* male fowl. A product of prudery and squeamishness. [Farmer]

get a wiggle on

To hurry. "You'll have to *get a wiggle on* to catch that train." Western Indiana. [Brown]

get the mitten

To be rejected or discarded by one's sweetheart. [Clapin] A phrase marking most characteristically the contrast between the free and easy manners of our day with those of past days, when the strongest term used for the painful occasion was to *give* and *get the mitten.* The latter word ought, however, always to be *mittens,* as the phrase is derived from the same use made of the French *mitaines,* which had to be accepted by the unsuccessful lover instead of the hand after which he aspired. [Schele de Vere]

get there with both feet

To be very successful. [Barrére]

gism

Strength; talent; genius; ability. Rhode Island. [Ellis] A synonym for energy, spirit. Probably from Dutch *geest.* [Farmer] Courage. [Tucker]

give one bringer

To give one severe punishment. "I'll *give you bringer* if you don't mind." Used in several comparative phrases, *hot as bringer, cold as bringer,* etc. Eastern Alabama. [Payne]

give one gowdy

To thrash soundly. [Thornton]

give the horrors

To terrify. The phrase "the horrors" is English, but "give the horrors" is, perhaps, American. [Thornton]

givy

Muggy. The weather is said to be *givy* when there is much moisture in it. South. [Dunglison]

gizzard-string

A supposed tendon in the stomach. "You like to a-popped you *gizzard-string*." Gullah, South Carolina. [Wentworth] "To break one's *puckering-string*" means to lose control of oneself and burst into hysterical giggling. West Brattleboro, Vermont. [Mead] "To burst the *liver-strings*," said of some violent exertion, as "If you laugh so hard you'll burst your *liver-strings*." Chicago. [Curtiss]

glasses off

To see a man with his *glasses off* is to see him informally, to converse with him in a familiar manner. College slang. [Weseen]

glom the grapevine

To steal clothes from a clothesline. This is the tramp's regular method of keeping in good linen. [Kane]

glory-hole

In mining, a hole which contains rich mineral deposits. Southwest. [Harvey] The strong room on old-time ships, where specie and treasure were kept. On modern steamships it is a slang term for the living-quarters of the cooks and stewards. Alongshore, it means a locker for odds and ends, a disorderly one being implied. [Colcord]

gnat's heel, gnat's toenail

Something quite small; also, perfectly. "It fitted to a *gnat's heel*." Missouri, southern Indiana. [Hanley] *Gnat's bris-*

tle, gnat's ear, a fine point. "He's got things down to a *gnat's bristle.*" Northwest Arkansas. [Carr] *Gnat's whistle,* a name of approbation for anything that is liked and regarded as desirable. [Weseen]

go-backs

Those who returned [to the East] with an evil report of the western country. [Thornton] In the mountains of Virginia, a baby is said to "have the *go-backs*" when its size does not correspond to what is expected. [Thornton] *Goback land,* land once cultivated but long since neglected. Kansas. [Ruppenthal]

go by water

To follow the sea as a calling. New Jersey coast. [Lee]

go-easter

Cowboy slang [for] a valise. So called because the cowboy seldom owns such an object till he buys one to go to a city, which is generally eastward. [Barrère]

golden eagles

Women's garments, especially panties. Golden eagle was a popular brand of flour; the sacks were often used for making garments, especially underclothing. Boontling language. [C. Adams]

gone coon

One in an awful fix, past praying for. This expression is said to have originated in the first American war with a spy who dressed himself in a raccoon skin and ensconced himself in a tree. An English rifleman, taking him for a veritable coon, leveled his piece at him, upon which he exclaimed, "Don't shoot. I'll come down myself. I know I'm a *gone coon.*" [Hotten]

goneness

A peculiar feeling in the stomach. Rhode Island. [Ellis] A

weakness; a word used by women. Central Connecticut. [Mead] *Gone by,* spoiled by decay. "The bananas are *gone by.*" Maine. [Maxfield]

gone to Texas

More than a generation ago, a common joke when an insolvent debtor, or any other loafer who had changed his home, wished to leave warning behind him where he had gone, he chalked upon his door the letters, "G. T. T." These letters . . . were understood to mean "gone to Texas." [Hale]

good as wheat

A phrase sometimes used instead of the more general one, "good as gold." It may possibly have originated in the usage of claiming rent or payment of debts in wheat. [Bartlett] *Good as the wheat,* trustworthy; very safe, especially in regards to financial matters. Southwestern Wisconsin. [Savage]

good-wooled

A man whose courage can be depended upon never to fail him is said to be *good-wooled.* [Farmer]

goody bread

Bread in which pieces of pork rind have been baked. A negro delicacy. [Farmer]

go on lays

A kind of limited partnership is, in the West, not unfrequently called *to go on lays.* The term is evidently derived from the slang term *lay,* which means some, a piece, etc., and is thus used in the North of England. Ordinarily the term is restricted to operations in which many participate and work jointly, as in whaling voyages and gold-diggings where all labor alike and each receives a share of the profits. [Schele de Vere]

goose-grabber

A Georgian; sometimes used of any backwoodsman. Eastern Alabama. [Payne]

goose hangs high

Everything is in fine order. "The goose honks high" is not heard except sporadically among the well-informed. Eastern Alabama. [Payne]

goose heaven

The abiding place of late lamented animal pets. Kansas. [Ruppenthal]

goose month

The month in which the spring migration of geese occurs, roughly mid-March to mid-April. Canada. [Scargill]

goozle

The larynx. Southern Illinois. [Rice] The throat. "I got up with a sore *goozle* this morning." Southeastern Missouri. [Crumb] To speak hoarsely; to swallow rapidly. *Goozler,* a boy whose voice is changing. North Carolina. [Cooper]

goozlum

Used of syrup, molasses, etc. at table. "Pass the *gazoolum* for these flapjacks." Nebraska. [Pound] Gravy. A long-winded play on the slang word *gooey,* thick or gummy in substance, probably originally from either *glue* or *gumbo.* [Irwin] *Alamagoozlum,* maple syrup. Sullivan and Orange counties, N.Y. [Wentworth]

gopher ranch

A ranch or farm having more gophers than cattle. Canada. [Scargill]

go short steps

For a man to go walking with a lady. Western Indiana. [Brown]

go short steps

gosling patch

The period in which a boy's voice is changing. *In the goslings,* in the period of changing voice. [Weseen]

gospel measure

Good measure; more than is asked for or in strictness required. Kansas. [Ruppenthal]

gospel-sharp

A Western term for a clergyman. [Farmer]

got a mash on

In love with. North Carolina. [Cooper]

government socks

The bare legs, or no socks at all. Snake County, Missouri. [Taylor]

grabble

In digging potatoes, to remove large ones without disturbing the small. Also, to steal potatoes without disturbing the hill. [Clapin]

grab-gutted

Greedy; selfish. Southern Illinois. [Rice]

granny doctor

Any obstetrician. North Carolina. [Kephart]

granny grunts

A stomach ache or menses. Eastern Alabama. [Payne]

grapevine telegraph

During the [Civil] War, exciting accounts of battles not fought and of victories not won were said to have been conveyed by *grapevine telegraph*. But the term was in earlier use meaning news conveyed in a mysterious manner. [Barrère]

grass freight

Goods shipped by bull team; called this because the motive power could eat their way to and from market. *Grass freight* was much slower but much cheaper than freight hauled by mule teams. West. [R. Adams]

grassoline

Cattle dung used as fuel. Kansas. [Ruppenthal]

gravels for my goose

Many expressions and allusions link the noun *gravel* with sexual contact. Ask a hillman where he is going and he replies, "To git some *gravels* for my goose," meaning that he is in search of sexual satisfaction. When a widow remarries, the neighbors say, "Well, Florrie has throwed away her *gravel-medicine*," a play upon the notion that frequent sexual intercourse cures diseases of the female kidney and bladder. To speak of a man's "turning over the *gravels*" means that he is in robust health, full of vigor—one who can urinate with such force that the stream of urine scatters pebbles. Ozarks. [Randolph & Wilson]

graveyard Christian

A churchgoer from dread of the hereafter. Kansas. [Ruppenthal] *Rice-Christians,* occupationless incapables who join the church for revenue only. [Ramsay]

grayslick

[This] word, belonging properly to the fishermen of Maine, means a state of the sea when the wind has died away and the water, unbroken by waves, assumes the familiar glassy appearance. The men will say, "We may just as well take to the oar, for we have gotten into a *grayslick.*" While the first part of the word refers to the dim but beautiful color, *slick* fully expresses the quiet, oleaginous condition of the sea in such places. [Schele de Vere]

grease-print

Mark Twain's first attempt to find a name for the new means of criminal identification, for which the term *finger-print* later found general acceptation. "Under this row of faint *grease-prints* . . ." —Mark Twain's *Pudd'nhead Wilson.* [Ramsay]

greasy luck

To wish a whaleman *greasy luck* meant to wish him a good voyage, with plenty of oil. Hence the Nantucketer uses uses it in well-wishes to his friends in any proposed venture. [Macy]

green fingers

A woman whose garden flourishes is said to have *green fingers.* Ozarks. [Randolph & Wilson]

griffe

The term seems pretty generally given to anything that is half-and-half. *Griffe* is, among the descendants of French settlers in Louisiana, applied to mulattoes, more especially to women. The fabulous *griffin* is represented as half eagle and half lion; and a cadet, half Indian and half English, is so called. *Griffins,* in England, is applied to the residue of a contract feast taken away by the contractor—half the buyer's and half the seller's. [Farmer]

grimp

One who makes many blunders. California. [Warnock]

grinsheep

A person who grins sheepishly. Northwest Arkansas. [Carr]

gripsack

A hand-bag or satchel. [Farmer & Henley]

groceteria

On the analogy of *cafeteria,* new words have been formed designating places conducted on the principle of self-service, such as *groceteria, caketeria, candyteria, pastreteria,* a pastry shop, and *drugeteria.* . . . This word probably originated in California, perhaps in Los Angeles, where the cafeteria first flourished. [Krapp] *Basketeria,* a grocery store organized on a self-serve basis, from the baskets provided, in which the customer collects his purchases; also so called from the fact that these institutions do not deliver. . . . *Cleaneteria,* a cleaning and dyeing establishment. California. [Lehman] *Casketeria,* a casket store. [Berrey]

grubstruck

Exhausted through hunger. Southern Illinois. [Rice]

gumbo French

A dialect or patois consisting in the main of strangely disguised and disfigured French words, with an admixture of English and a few genuine African terms. [Farmer] *Gombo,* the French dialect of the Louisiana negro. Mississippi Valley. [McDermott]

gump

A stolen chicken; a mud-baked hen. The chicken is baked thus: It is first cleaned internally; then wet clay is packed about the body without plucking it, and the bird is baked in fire made in a hole in the ground with embers packed all around it. In about an hour the bird is removed; the hardened mud-pack is cracked with a kick and then lifted off, the feathers adhering to it. Hobo slang. [Goldin]

gut-hammer

The dinner gong at a construction camp. [Kane]

guttler

A greedy eater. Virginia. [Green]

The people inhabiting the rural districts of the Southwestern states have . . . adopted many words and phrases which are not found in Webster's dictionary or sanctioned by any of our grammarians. They have also taken the liberty of changing the pronunciation of many words in such a manner, and applying them in such novel ways that it is almost impossible for one not familiar with these peculiarities to comprehend their meanings in ordinary conversation.

—American Col. Randolph Barnes Marcy's
Thirty Years of Army Life on the Border (1866)

Hail Columbia

A severe punishment or scolding. "You'll get *Hail Columbia* when your mother comes home." Western New York, the South. [Bowen]

haily over

A children's game of ball played as follows: The players choose sides and take positions on opposite sides of a barn. One player throws the ball over the barn, crying out, "Haily over," perhaps a corruption for "Hail ye! Over!" One of the opposing players tries to catch it and then tags one of his opponents with the ball. The player tagged has to change sides. The side wins which gains all the players. Eastern Maine, western Connecticut. [Carr]

half a quarter

One eighth of a mile; a rather common unit of measure. "He lives *half a quarter* from here." Southeastern Missouri. [Crumb]

half-dime

The only other coin peculiar to the United States is the dime—a silver coin of the value of ten cents—and the *half-dime*. In the [1600s], dimes . . . were apt to represent all the money property of a person, and a young lady was said to "have the dimes" when she was reputed rich. [Schele de Vere]

half-leg high

Knee high. "My corn is *half-leg high*." Southeastern Missouri. [Crumb]

half-saved

A *half-saved* person is a weak-minded or shallow-brained individual. A New England phrase which is provincial in England. [Farmer]

half-sole yourself

To refill one's glass when it is only half empty. Ozarks. [Randolph & Wilson]

half-widow

The term is, in New England and New York, applied to a woman whose husband is shiftless, and fails in his duty to provide for her necessities. [Farmer]

hallelujah peddler

A minister; one who tries to sell salvation. . . . *Heaven rancher,* a minister of the gospel; one who preaches about salvation and Heaven, as often as not with skyward gestures. *Salvation rancher,* a preacher, mission attaché, or evangelist. [Irwin] *Jackleg preacher,* a minister completely lacking in professional training, who usually preaches "on the side." Texas. [Atwood] *Bible-puncher,* a preacher. *Bible-pounder* is a variant. West. . . . *Fire escape,* a revivalist; a preacher. [Weseen] *Fire insurance agent,* a preacher. New England. [Hanford]

hamfatter

A recent name in some quarters of New York for a second-rate dude or masher. [Farmer] *Dude hamfatter,* sarcastic allusion to pork-raisers. A large number are located not a hundred miles from Chicago. [Barrère]

hammerhard

Iron or steel hardened by hammering. [Webster]

hand-glasses

Eye-glasses and spectacles are so called in New York. [Farmer]

hand in one's checks

An Americanism for dying, giving up the ghost, meaning properly to make your will and settle your earthly affairs. All over the United States it is the custom at German restaurants to give a certain amount of credit to known regular patrons, who now and again are asked to *hand in their checks,* or vouchers, for settlement. [Johnson]

hand shoes

Gloves. *Hand sox,* gloves or mittens. Pacific Northwest. [McCulloch]

handsome thing

"To do the *handsome thing*" is a Yankee's effusive way of saying that he will be generous, or very polite. Perhaps the nearest English equivalent is being "civil." [Farmer]

handy as a pocket in a shirt

A New England simile for convenient. [Farmer]

hang the landlady

To decamp without payment; applied to moonshining practices of all descriptions. An equivalent is "to stand off the tailor." [Farmer]

hang up one's fiddle

To give up. [Bartlett] *Higher 'n Bolley's fiddle,* very drunk. Neglected; out of use. A local man named Bolley was a fine violin player, but for some inexplicable reason he suddenly "hung his fiddle high," gave up his musical activities. Boontling language. [C. Adams]

happifying

Making happy. This strange word is sometimes heard from our pulpits, and a clerical friend informs me that he has met with it in some of our printed sermons. [Pickering] A barbarous term of hybrid origin—half Latin and half English. [Dunglison]

happy as a clam at high tide

Very happy. New Hampshire, Connecticut. *Happy as ducks in Arizona,* very unhappy. Arizona. [Hanford]

hat of woods

A low growth of trees on the top of a small hill. Newfoundland. [Devine]

Hawkin's whetstone

Inferior rum. Mr. Hawkins, a one-time zealous temperance advocate . . . raised the ire of some Western men, thirsty souls who loved their liquor. . . . They, in retaliation, sought to turn the tables on the temperance reformer by branding a low-class rum with his name. This cheap retort served for a time amongst these boon companions, but the expression is rarely used nowadays. [Farmer]

heading

Pillow, bolster, etc. "If you haven't *heading* enough,

I'll get you another pillow." Southeastern Missouri. [Crumb]

hearn

Hearn, the old adjective-participle for *heard,* is quite frequently heard where old English most prevails, in New England and Virginia. [Schele de Vere]

hear the hoot owl

To have many and varied experiences; to get drunk. West. [R. Adams]

hearty as a buck

A hunter's phrase, now in very common use. [Bartlett]

heater piece

As applied to land, a triangular or wedge-shaped piece of ground. This New England phrase is thought to be derived from the similarity of shape to the heaters of box-irons used by housewives. [Farmer]

heave down

To give up, as smoking. Newfoundland. [England]

hedgehopper

A professional swindler of accident insurance companies who continually moves from town to town in order to escape exposure. . . . A clever *hedgehopper* is ever on the alert for open manhole covers, badly lighted hallways, broken stairs, torn carpets, etc., providing the opportunities for him to feign injury. [Goldin]

heel of the day

The last part of the afternoon. Newfoundland. [England]

he-huckleberry

A variety of huckleberry, the fruit of which is twice the size of the ordinary kind. Ozarks. [Randolph]

height social

A party to which one pays an admission fee proportioned to one's height. Northwest Arkansas. [Carr]

hell a-popping

A tremendous row or dispute, no doubt from the propensity of those who use . . . their six shooters at the slightest provocation. [Barrère]

hello-girl

A young woman telephone operator. "The humblest *hello-girl* . . . could teach the high est dutchess." —Mark Twain's *Connecticut Yankee*. [Ramsay]

Hello, the house!

Used to attract the attention of someone indoors. Ohio, Wisconsin. [Wentworth]

henskin show

A clear day. There was once an expression in the Olympic Peninsula area, "put on light clothes, boys, it's a *henskin day.*" Pacific Northwest. [McCulloch]

hen-waller-jostle

When anything is done in a very lively manner it is done like a *hen-waller-jostle*—that is, as a hen lies in the sun in the dust, and vigorously shakes herself. Kentucky. [Combs]

heredities

That which is derived by hereditary transmission. [Ramsay]

hicapooka

An unnamable or indescribable disease or general disability; also *hicapookum*. Eastern Alabama. [Payne]

hickey

A degree or two short of being drunk—the good-tempered roseate stage. [Farmer]

higgs

Money; a roll of bills; affluence. Special application of plural of *hig,* dollar, to mean money in the collective. *Higgy,* wealthy, having money. *Higgery,* a bank. Boontling language. [C. Adams]

highbinder

The name given to men employed as spies upon the Chinese. This is specially the case in California, where the Chinese trouble has been most acute. [Farmer] A set of organized villains in New York City; also, later, the term was applied to Chinese gangs on the Pacific Coast. [Thornton]

High Dutchers

A cant term for skates, the blade of which is curled up high in the front. [Schele de Vere] "The Germans, or *High Dutchers,* as they were called to distinguish them from the original or Low Dutch colonists, were a very peculiar people." —James Fenimore Cooper's *The Pioneers,* 1823.

higher than Gilderoy's kite

Very high. "He knocked him *higher than Gilderoy's kite.*" Southwestern Wisconsin. [Savage]

high hook

The one who catches the largest or the greatest quantity of fish. Rhode Island. [Ellis]

hightantrabogus

A noisy good time, as in "raisin' hightantrabogus." Plymouth, Massachusetts. [Briggs]

higulcion flips

An imaginary ailment. Texas. [Farmer & Henley]

hike yourself off

The expression *hike yourself off* is used to an intruder, or to hasten one on an errand. Southern Illinois. [Rice]

hindhouse

An outhouse. [Atkinson]

hindside

Behind. "The broom is *hindside* the door." Cape Cod. [Chase]

hippers

Nails used to fasten trousers to a shirt; from *hip*. Newfoundland. [England]

hippoed

Subject to some imaginary ailment. . . . Hypochondria was vulgarly called "the hypo" in England as early as 1711. Ozarks. [Randolph] *Hipped*, melancholy; sad. Newfoundland. [Devine]

hippoed

hitch along

To move along on a seat without rising. Cape Cod. [Chase]

hit the maples

To bowl. [Weseen]

hog-killing time

A lively time; a jollification. From the old-fashioned custom of having a party in connection with the butchering of hogs. "He and some of his cronies happened to get together and they did have a *hog-killing time!*" Southeastern Missouri. [Crumb]

hog-Latin

A strange-sounding language, especially bad Latin or an intentionally distorted form of English used for purposes of deception or display. [Craigie] Gibberish invented by schoolchildren; "dog-Latin." Eastern Alabama. [Payne]

hog-meat

Pork; the word *pork* is seldom used in the South. South-eastern Missouri. [Crumb]

hog-tight and horse-high

Always used together, of fences that are sufficient to restrain trespassing stock. Maryland. [Bartlett]

hold one's potato

To be quiet. Georgia. [Thornton]

holus bolus

Violence; energy. "He goes at it *holus bolus*." Martha's Vineyard, Massachusetts. [Rees]

holy laugh

A laugh uttered in a state of religious hysteria or fervor, usually at camp meetings. [Craigie] Hysterical laughter was at first sporadic, but in 1803 we find the "holy laugh" introduced systematically as a part of worship. [Davidson] The preacher, in the midst of a fervent prayer, will all of a sudden burst out into a loud boisterous laugh. . . . The most godly of his brethren join with him. This is called the *holy laugh*. —*Maryland Historical Magazine,* 1906.

holy tone

A method of utterance, often used in their sermons by Primitive Baptist preachers, in which the sound "ah" occurs at the end of each breath pause, and the taking of fresh breath is intentionally made audible. Also *holy whine*. "Often the preacher had no idea what he would say from one 'ah' to the next. The *holy tone* had charms for the audience, and they preferred such a sermon to that learned by a learned college president." —Everett Dick's *The Dixie Frontier,* 1948. [Mathews]

homesteader's fiddle

A crosscut saw. Canada. [Scargill]

homologize

To assimilate. [Thornton]

hoopendaddy

Indefinite expression, like *thingumbob,* usually referring to food. "Pass me some of that *hoopendaddy.*" Nebraska. [Pound]

hoopsisaw

A rustic or low dance, and a lively tune adapted to it. Inferior lively music is sometimes called "hoopsisaw music." Pennsylvania Dutch. [Haldeman]

hootsle

Small, contracted. "They lived in a miserable, *hootsle* way." Also a small person or thing. [Wentworth] In Pennsylvania, a peach dried without removing the stone. [From] German *hotzel,* a dried fruit. [Haldeman]

Hoover pork

Rabbit meat. This is a reference to the lean years when Herbert Hoover was president, and many families could get no meat except rabbits. Ozarks. [Randolph & Wilson]

hopine

A name given to malt liquor which for all practical purposes is genuine beer, but which is so called to evade the Provisions of the Prohibition Act. Iowa is one of the so-called Prohibition states, a fact which will explain the following quotation [from] *Texas Siftings* (1888): "They sell a drink out there called *hopine,* which experts can't tell from beer, but the sale of which is not a violation of the liquor law." [Farmer]

horny-handed

Having the hands hardened or callused by labor. Same as *horny-fisted*. [Whitney]

horse and horse

Even; originally applied to horses which in running a race come in side by side; or as the phrase goes, "neck and neck." [Bartlett]

horseback opinion

One given hastily without consulting the authorities. [Thornton]

horse boat

A boat moved by horses; a new species of ferry-boat. [Webster]. A boat propelled by horses working a treadmill that drove the paddle-wheel(s). [Scargill] "They wended their way to the ferry just in time to see the *horse boat* come splashing into port, the four horses plodding their unprogressive journey on the revolving wheel." —R. E. Robinson's *Uncle Lisha's Outing,* 1898.

horse drama

A form of drama in which trained horses are used. [Mathews]

horse editor

In the United States, not only the manager or proprietor and director of a newspaper is called an "editor," but also all who write for it, the chief reporter being the "city editor" and the reviewer the "literary editor," while the gentleman who furnishes the sporting news is sometimes facetiously termed the *horse editor.* [Barrère]

horse-pint

A large pint. *Horse-quart,* a large quart. West Virginia. "I

pulled a *horse-quart* o' moonshine from my saddlebags."
—Jesse Stuart's *Men of the Mountains*, 1941. [Wentworth]

horse-pint

horse-proud

Adjective used of a man who has pride in his blooded stock. Similar words are used made up with names of other animals, as *hog-proud*. New Jersey. [Lee]

houp la

This exclamation on the part of a circus ringmaster, as a signal for an equestrienne to leap over horizontal barriers or through paper hoops, has been derived from the Californian stage drivers' ejaculation to their horses. [Johnson]

hour by sun

An hour after sunrise or before sunset. [Rollins] The measurement of time by the height of the sun is still quite common. "The sun was *two hours high* when I left home, and I aim to get back by an *hour by sun*." Southeastern Missouri. [Crumb] In the middle of the seventeenth century there were few clocks on [Cape Cod]. Time was reckoned as *suncoming, sun-an-hour, sun-two-hours*, then *midday, sun-four-*

hours-up, sun-three-hours-up, sunset, sober light (twilight), *first-hour-night, second-hour-night*. [Tallman] "How high's the sun?" What time is it? Used by the generation born in the early nineteenth century. New Hampshire. [Carr]

housekeep, roomkeep

Housekeep, as a verb, has firmly established itself in American speech. The new word, *to roomkeep*, arising from the exigency which forces impoverished Southern families to content themselves with renting a few rooms and keeping house in them, has not yet obtained currency. [Schele de Vere]

how-come-you-so

Pregnant. "She's *how-come-you-so*." Southwestern Wisconsin. [Savage]

how d'ye rise?

A Western salutation meaning *how do you get along*. Rhode Island. [Ellis]

howsomever

However. Georgia. [Sherwood]

hubbly

Rough. "The road was *hubbly*." Cape Cod. [Chase]

huckery

Cheating, especially in love. Central Pennsylvania. [Shoemaker]

huck it

To walk; from *hucks*, feet. Maine, Northern New Hampshire. [England]

huckleberry above the persimmon

To be a *huckleberry above one's persimmon* is a Southern phrase meaning to excel. [Bartlett] *Above one's huckleberry*, beyond one's ability; out of one's reach. [Farmer & Henley]

huckleberry chowder

"Odd as *huckleberry chowder*" is an expressive localism used as a simile for extreme eccentricity. Nantucket. [Macy]

hum box

This term, which in England for a very long time stood for a pulpit among thieves and their associates, is in America applied by the same class of people to an auctioneer's desk. [Farmer]

hunker

Knee. "Get down on your *hunkers*." Southern Illinois. [Rice]

hurry stumps

To hasten. Louisiana. [Parry]

huzzlecoo

A flirtation. [Weseen]

hweegeed

[Deformed.] "It was all *hweegeed* out of shape." Nebraska. [Pound]

hyphenated American

An Irish-American, a German-American, or other naturalized citizen of the States. [Sandilands]

'Tis strange to see how this humour prevails, even among the lower class of the people here. They will talk so pointedly about justification, sanctification, adoption, regeneration, repentance, free grace, reprobation, original sin, and a thousand other such pretty chimerical knickknacks as if they had done nothing but studied divinity all their life-time. . . . To talk this dialect in our parts would be like Greek, Hebrew, or Arabick.

—Scottish physician Alexander Hamilton's
Itinerarium, Being a Narrative of a Journey from Annapolis,
Maryland (1744), commenting on the commonplace
Connecticut subject of religion, recorded August 27 of that year

ice candle

Icicle. Newfoundland. [England]

ice cream shot

An easy hunting shot. In the days when ice cream was brought to sporting camps in large wooden tubs, packed with ice and salt, the tubs were returned to town for credit. The choreboy would dump the salt brine from them in a certain place behind camp to attract deer, whose delight in finding salt is well known. Then, in hunting season, a sport who has not shot his deer but had come to the end of his outing would be given an *ice cream shot* on his last day. . . . The term is used to describe any easy shot, as when a buck stands side[ways] about twenty yards away, whether salted or not. It is also applied to easy scores in athletics. Maine. [Gould]

ice-worm cocktail

A cocktail, originally served in the Klondike, having as a basic ingredient ice-worms—actually bits of spaghetti or macaroni. [From] *ice-worm,* a mythical creature born as a practical joke in the Yukon during the Klondike gold rush. [Scargill]

icken

In the patter of low life in New York, *icken* means oak, the tree itself being called *icken baum.* This is evidently a corruption of the German *eiche,* an oak. [Farmer]

illy

Illy, frequently charged upon American writers as an unpardonable sin, is used by some of the older English writers, though sparingly. It has excited much controversy, and while there is no well-founded objection to the use of the word, it has not been sanctioned by the consent of the people. In Texas the word *ill* has the curious signification of immoral, and an "ill fellow" means a man of bad habits. [Barrère] *Ill* is equally an adverb and adjective, and hence *illy,* to say the least of it, is unnecessary. [Dunglison]

improved Britisher

An immigrant from the British Isles, especially an Englishman, who has been in Canada long enough to have lost some of his native shortcomings. [Scargill]

Indian ladder

A ladder made of a small tree by trimming it so as to leave only a few inches of each branch as a support for the foot. [Bartlett]

Indian signboard

The bleached shoulder bone of a buffalo, commonly seen upon the plains in the early days. The Indians painted messages on these bones. West. [R. Adams]

indoor aviator

An elevator operator. [Berrey]

in fourteen languages

To a very great extent or a very high degree, as "I was sick *in fourteen languages.*" [Weseen]

inheaven

A badly-made and unmeaning word manufactured by "Boston Transcendentalists," and unfortunately, often used by careless writers in the sense of to lift us up to heaven. "Such music is well calculated to *inheaven* us." [Schele de Vere]

inkle

To attend [a gathering] without invitation. "I'm going over to the party and *inkle* in." West Virginia. [Wentworth]

inn-holder

An innkeeper. The word is traced back to 1464. It is probably obsolete even in the United States. [Thornton]

in slings

Delayed; deferred; unfinished or in suspense, like a barrel suspended in the slings while being hoisted from one place to another. Newfoundland. [Devine]

in spots

In spots, one of the suggestive and graphic phrases which the West originates every now and then for a shortlived popularity, means *occasionally* or *here and there.* The phrase "He is clever *in spots*" gives a man credit for fragmentary ability, and when a poor hunter comes to a town or a digging where lodgings are scarce, he is ready to "sleep in spots," i.e. wherever he can find a shelter. [Schele de Vere]

in Texas

Anywhere; the most remote place. "I'd know that hat *in Texas*." Northwest Arkansas. [Carr]

in the suck

Unpaid. "[He] left them *in the suck* for his board." North Carolina. [Eliason]

in the suds

An Americanism for being unprepared to receive visitors. The allusion is to a washerwoman with her hands in the soapsuds. [Johnson] In the thick of things, especially in a social way, as "She's right *in the suds*." Nantucket. [Macy]

in the woodbox

To be "sick a-bed *in the woodbox*" is to be laid up with a minor complaint which, although distressing, doesn't put you to bed. To be flabbergasted by sudden bad news is to be "knocked clean *into the woodbox*" by surprise. Maine. [Gould]

intime

Friendly; [from] French *intime* [intimate]. College slang. "Mary is certainly getting *intime* with Jane." [Savage] The true inwardness of a thing is its true purpose, the object aimed at, its exact drift. This is one of the fashionable canting phrases of the day. [Farmer]

Irishman's crossing

An Americanism for the mode of many people anxious to cut corners by crossing and recrossing the street, by which process one's way is actually made longer. [Johnson]

Irish pasture

A state of coma. "I socked that fellow into the *Irish pasture*." [Kane]

iron-man

A silver dollar. Pacific Northwest. [Lehman] *Iron-dollar,* a silver dollar. Kansas. [Ruppenthal]

I should smile

In this phrase, a strong accent is laid on *should.* It comes from such expressions as "Well, I *should* think!" which are often left incomplete, but which when completed would be, "that he ought to be ashamed," or "that people would know better," &c. Its general meaning is an intimation of surprise or mild contempt. It is much used by women and is believed to have originated in the suburbs of Boston or in Brooklyn. [Barrère]

itch neemer

A person who no longer craves alcoholic beverages; the condition of being free from such desire after a period of addiction. Combination of *itch* and phonetically reshaped *no more.* Boontling language. [C. Adams]

izickity

An exclamation. Northwest Arkansas. [Carr]

The Americans dwell upon their words when they speak—a custom arising, I presume, from their cautious calculating habits; and they have always more or less of a nasal twang. I once said to a lady, "Why do you drawl out your words in that way?"

"Well," she replied, "I'd drawl all the way from Maine to Georgia rather than *clip* my words as you English people do."

—English naval captain Frederick Marryat's
A Diary in America, With Remarks on Its Institutions (1839)

Jack White

A shirt-tail. "*Jack White* is out of jail" means that there is a hole in the seat of one's trousers. Cape Cod. [Chase] *Letter in the post office,* an expression current among boys denoting that the seat of the trousers is so out of repair that the shirt-tail is visible. Western Connecticut. [Babbitt] *Letter in the post-office,* a flying shirt-tail. [Farmer & Henley]

jag

A load. [Fearon] An Americanism for drunkenness. "He's got a *jag* on," he's on a drinking bout. [Johnson] A man who walks unsteadily, owing to intoxication, is said to "have a *load on.*" [Barrère]

jake

A rustic lout. "These country *jakes* won't even think of that." —Mark Twain's *Huckleberry Finn*. [Ramsay]

jamoke

Coffee; without a doubt from the two words indicating the sections of the world—Java and Mocha—from which much of the coffee comes. *Joe* [is] probably a contraction of *jamoke*. [Irwin]

January gravestone

Cold as the north side of a *January gravestone* by starlight. [Lowell]

janusmug

An intermediary between the thief and the receiver [of stolen goods]. Like the two-faced mythical deity Janus, the *janusmug* turns first to the one side and then to the other. [Farmer]

jargle

To emit a harsh or shrill sound. [Webster]

jawsmith

One who works with his jaw, especially a loud-mouthed demagogue. [Whitney]

jazzicist

A performer who produces jazz. Theater slang. [Weseen]

jemmy

Spruce; neat; well-dressed. *Jemminess,* spruceness; neatness. [Colange] When a boy has not brushed his hair and it stands on end, he is called a *Jemmy Jed*. In the old American editions of Mother Goose's nursery rhymes, Jemmy Jed is represented in a rude woodcut as rushing from a shed with his hair on end. [Barrère]

jerkwater

Originally a railroad word, probably from a water tank

which was "jerked" for the engines. Attributive, designating things as small townish or of no significance. [Craigie] A train on a branch railway. Northwest Arkansas. "Has the *jerkwater* come in yet?" [Carr]

jerp

A small quantity. The word is most often used in reference to sweets. "She shore does like a leetle *jerp* o' sugar in her bread." *By jerps* is a common expression of astonishment. Ozarks. [Randolph]

jibble

To cut into small pieces. Asked how to cook squash, a woman answered, "You just take and *jibble* 'em up, an' then boil 'em." Ozarks. [Randolph & Wilson]

jiglets

His jiglets, a derisively contemptuous [mock-royal] form of address. [Farmer]

jimjams

A violently upset or disturbed feeling. "Her talking so long gave me the *jimjams*." Nebraska. [Pound]

jimpsecute

In the Texas vernacular, this is used when a young man goes to pay his devoirs to the fair one, to signify the object of his attention. She, on the other hand, calls her lover a "juicy-spicy." [Barrère]

jitney dance

A public dance in which a charge of five cents is made for each dance. [Weseen] *Jitney,* a five-cent piece. A bus on which the fare is five cents. [Tucker] *Dime party,* a social affair, entry to which required a donation of a dime, usually for charity. Canada. [Scargill]

jizzicked

Anything so far gone that repairs are pointless. "That

washing machine is so *jizzicked* that you might's well buy a new one." Maine. [Gould]

joe darter

A very fine or excellent thing; a shrewd or smart person. "He's a *joe darter* when it comes to trading." Eastern Alabama. [Payne]

joggling-board

"A *joggling-board* is the latest contrivance for exercise that has made its appearance in these parts, and it is liable to become the poor man's horse. . . . One sits on the board, waves his arms up and down, and then *joggles,* the board sending him up and down on the board, as a horse." —*Kansas City Star,* August 18, 1904. [Thornton]

John Davis, ready John

Money itself has in the United States, as in England, probably more designations than any other object—liquor alone excepted—many of which are purely whimsical, while others may be traced back to the material of which coins are made. Among the less generally known terms are *John Davis,* or the *ready John*—sometimes simply *John* or *ready*—*spondulics, dooteroomus* (often shortened into *doot*), *tow, wad, hardstuff* (or *hard*), *dirt, shinplasters* (or simply *plasters*) *wherewith, shadscales* (or *scales*) *dyestuffs, charms,* and also the more modern designation of *stamps,* all of which are . . . considered as Americanisms. [Schele de Vere]

Johnny-at-the-rathole

"To play *Johnny-at-the-rathole,*" to pry into other people's affairs; to eavesdrop. Nebraska. [Pound]

jole

The common way of writing [spelling phonetically] according to the sound. [Schele de Vere]

joog

Slight sign of force, energy, life; usually after a negative. "There's not a *joog* left in him." Newfoundland. [Story]

josh

A word shouted at the New York Stock Exchange to wake up a sleepy member. [Bartlett] A member drops asleep, worn out it maybe by long nights and feverish daily wrestlings with bull or bear. "Josh, Josh, Josh," comes roaring from a dozen leathern lungs, and the broker lifts his head and rubs his eyes, startled from slumber by the traditional rallying cry. [Medbery]

journalier

A day-laborer, principally in agriculture. Mississippi Valley. [McDermott]

jubbers

Suspicious. "I'm *jubbers* of that fellow." Southern Indiana. [Hanley]

Judas-steer

One used at slaughterhouses and so trained that he leads other cattle to slaughter. He is then returned to lead others. West. [R. Adams]

juice road

An electric railway, usually an interurban line, on which the motive power is "juice." [Irwin]

jularker

In the long ago, a male sweetheart was a *jularker* and his sweetheart was a *jusem sweet*. North Carolina. [Cooper]

Authorities differ between themselves—and often *with* themselves—when asked to set down in plain scientific terms the marks which distinguish vagrant words of slang from correct and orthodox English. . . . The borderland between slang and the Queen's English is an ill-defined territory, the limits of which have never been clearly mapped out. It is, therefore, not without hesitation that I have ventured to explore this "Dark Continent" of the World of Words.

—Englishman John S. Farmer, in the
"Prefatory Note" to his *Slang and Its Analogues* (c. 1890)

kedge

In good health or spirits. [Fearon] Brisk. "How do you do to-day? I am pretty *kedge*." [Bartlett] It is used only in a few of the country towns of New England. [Pickering]

keeping-room

Keeping-room, instead of *drawing-room*—almost universal in New England—is found in Norfolk and Suffolk, England, proving once more how many of the settlers must have come from the eastern counties of England. [Schele de Vere]

keep school

To teach school mechanically, without being interested in

the profession. . . . *School-keeper,* one who *keeps,* but does not teach, school. Northwest Arkansas. [Carr]

kelumpus

An onomatopoeticism. *Kelumpus* is supposed to be an imitation of the sound made by one heavy body upon another. [Farmer]

Kentucky colonel

A bogus colonel. After the American Civil War, it is alleged, nearly every man in Kentucky was either a captain, a colonel, or a general. [Sandilands] This title [colonel] is conferred upon prominent mountain men without any reference to military service. Nearly every auctioneer is an honorary colonel, as are many country lawyers and bankers. Maine. [Maxfield]

Kentucky treat

Same as *Dutch treat.* Louisiana. [Routh]

kerzip

To be "off one's *kerzip,*" to be out of one's mind. Eastern Alabama. [Payne]

kidlet

Diminutive of *kid,* child. Nebraska, Pennsylvania, Kansas. [Pound]

kidleybenders

Ice which undulates under the feet of a skater. [Farmer & Henley] *Rubber ice,* ice, as on a creek, that bends but does not break under one's weight. Michigan. [Wentworth]

kilgubbin

A low or poor neighborhood. Chicago. [Curtiss]

kilockety

To travel by train. Imitative of the sound of metal wheels on rails. [Companion term of] *kiloppety,* to travel by a horse-drawn vehicle or on horseback. Imitative of the sound of shod hooves on a roadway. Boontling language. [C. Adams]

kilockety

kind of hair-pin

A man . . . in the odd expression "That's the *kind of hair-pin* I am," popular about 1880. It is derived from a fanciful resemblance of the human figure to a double-tyned hair-pin, just as in Shakespeare's time a thin man was compared to a forked radish. In America, the simile is popularly extended to clothes-[pins] and tongs. [Barrère] "That's the *kind of hair-pin* I am" originated in New York. [Farmer]

king's ex

A call, abbreviated, of "king's excuse," used by children to stop a game for a moment. In playing "base," when a boy falls down, and to keep from being caught, he usually says *King's ex!* which serves him as a protection. [Clapin]

kinnery

Kin-folks. Eastern Alabama. [Payne]

kirkbuzzer

A thief whose specialty is to ply in churches. [Matsell]

Moll-buzzer, a pickpocket who preys upon women. [Kane]

kiss-curl

A name for the little curls on the ladies' temples, also known as "beau-catchers." [Schele de Vere]

kiss the cook

At table, when one takes the last piece on a dish he must be willing to *kiss the cook.* Eastern Alabama. [Payne]

kiss the dog

To face a victim while in the act of picking his pocket. [Goldin]

Klondiker

An heiress-hunter. Louisiana. [Routh] *Klondike,* a period of good income; a time of plenty. From the Klondike gold rush of the 1890s. Newfoundland. [Story]

knight of the yardstick

A dry-goods retail clerk. [Bartlett]

knowledge box

A schoolhouse. Pacific Northwest. [Harvey]

know one's oil

To be well informed. Some of the numerous variants are *know one's bananas* . . . and *know one's beans.* [Weseen]

It is well known that many words and expressions have been preserved, and are yet in common use in America, but which have become obsolete in England. . . . Such obsolete words and expressions, whenever they occur in Shakespeare are, of course, understood at first sight by the American reader, while to make them intelligible to the English reader they appear to require notes.

—American medical doctor Charles Woodward Stearns's
The Shakespeare Treasury of Wisdom (1869)

ladies' walk, gentlemen's walk

A privy. This absurd piece of squeamishness is common at hotels and at railroad stations. [Bartlett] When a caller asked for the daughter of the house, an old granny said, "Just set down young man. She's out a-teasin' the cat." Granny meant that the girl had gone to an outdoor privy. Ozarks. [Randolph & Wilson]

lady-caller

An American expression explained by a quotation from the *St. James Gazette*: "A *lady-caller* is a cultivated and presentable woman nicely dressed who takes a salary for distributing cards for fashionable folk, and as we presume from the accomplishments demanded of her, even occasionally makes actual calls instead of the lady who employs her, and who, by a social fiction, is supposed to be calling." [Barrère]

Lady of the Snows

A name bestowed upon Canada by Rudyard Kipling. [Sandilands]

lagniappe

Something thrown in, over and above; good measure. "We picked up one excellent word worth traveling to New Orleans to get; a nice limber, expressive, handy word—*lagniappe*. They pronounce it lanny-*yap*. . . . If the waiter in the restaurant stumbles and spills a gill of coffee down the back of your neck, he says 'For lagniappe, sah,' and gets you another cup without charge." —Mark Twain's *Life on the Mississippi*. [Farmer]

land-broker

An undertaker. [Matsell]

land poor

Maine farmers unable to work all the land they own are said to be *land poor*. Maine. [Gould]

landwash

The seashore between high and low tide marks, washed by the sea; occasionally the shore of a pond or river. Newfoundland. [Story]

languishment

This disease [pulmonary consumption] . . . they call a *languishment*. Nantucket Island. [Pickering]

laprobe

A napkin. Kansas. [Ruppenthal]

large blue kind

This very eccentric expression, signifying magnitude

and intensity, seems to have been suggested by blue bottle flies, which are larger and more disliked than any others. A particularly bad humbug, or lie, is sometimes described as being "one of the large blue kind." [Barrère]

largest village

It is a standing joke that Philadelphia is the "largest village" in the United States. [Thornton]

last button on Jacob's coat

The last thing; also "the last pea in the dish." Eastern Alabama. [Payne]

last year's bird's-nest

In the expression "He hasn't any more sense than *last year's bird's-nest,*" his head is as empty as last year's bird's-nest. Northwest Arkansas. [Carr]

laugh fat

For *laugh fat* the *Oxford English Dictionary* notes a reflexive use, "laugh themselves fat," but it is also used with a personal pronoun as the object, as in "They pretty near *laughed* me *fat.*" North Carolina. [Eliason]

lean on your own breakfast

An imperative phrase [meaning] "Sit up; don't lean on me." Western New York. [Bowen]

lean toward Jones's

To slant, be out of plumb. A carpenter's expression. "That wall *leans toward Jones's.*" Northwest Arkansas. [Carr]

leather-ears

A person slow of comprehension. Cape Cod. [Chase]

leatherbread

A pancake. [Wentworth]

leather medal

An imaginary reward for stupidity. [Thornton]

lecture-day

Used in New England for *holiday*, from the custom of excusing boys from going to school on those week-days when there was a public lecture. "All constables may and shall from time to time duly make search throughout the limits of their townes upon Lord's dayes and lecture-days in times of exercise . . . for all offenders against this law." —*Massachusetts Colony Laws*, 1660. [Pickering]

left-legged

Clumsy in walking. [Berrey] Incompetent as a dancer. Theater slang. [Weseen]

leg drama

A ballet. Theatres where stage-dancing forms a prominent feature of the entertainment are similarly called *leg-shops*. [Farmer]

leg of the law

A lawyer; also "limb of the law." [Bartlett]

leg-stretcher

To *take a leg-stretcher* is to take a drink. Obviously from the fact that to stretch one's legs more often than not is synonymous with walking to the refreshment bar and back again. Somewhat akin is the excuse of "going out to see a man" when leaving one's seat between the acts at a theatre. Both these and many other phrases are regarded as an excuse for a glass. [Farmer] This arose from the common traveller's exclamation, while the stagecoach was waiting for the mails, "I'll get off a bit and stretch my legs." Far West. [Johnson]

leg-stretcher

let the hoe handle suck

To loaf and talk while one is supposed to be working. "There he is, *lettin' the hoe handle suck*." Southwestern Wisconsin. [Savage]

lickety whittle

Recklessly fast. Cape Cod. [Chase] *Lickety-brindle,* very swiftly. Western Indiana. [Brown]

lids

The cover or binding of a book. "No Sir, you caint find it nowhar 'twixt th' *lids* o' th' Book." The word "Book" in the Ozark mountains means the King James version of the Bible. [Randolph]

lig robber

A thief who hides under a bed or in a closet until a woman is alone in the house, when she is robbed and possibly assaulted. *Lig* is the old cant word for a bed. [Irwin]

lightning changers, lightning shifters

Women thieves who can in a minute, by adroit and inge-nious manipulation, change their dress in a most extraordinary manner. There is a dress worn by women of this class in Paris, consisting of all the garments in one, so made that in a few seconds the whole may be slipped off [exposing another]. [Barrère]

like a book

Thoroughly; accurately. "She sang like a nightengale and talked *like a book*." [Thornton]

like a father-in-law to a dog

To talk to anyone "like a father-in-law to a dog" is to give them a good scolding. Cape Cod. [Chase]

like a frozen-toed chicken

Used to describe a gait in walking. Southwestern Wisconsin. [Savage]

like sixty

Like everything; very badly. "That child cuts up *like sixty*." [Bowen] For some occult reason, this number is used by many to supply the lack of a ready comparison, as "He scolded *like sixty* because the job wasn't done." [Bartlett]

like Texas

"It rained *like Texas*." Southeastern Ohio. [Parry] *Like hell for Texas,* in a hurry. Western Indiana. [Brown]

limb

Limb, instead of *leg,* [is] one of the evidences of the false prudishness prevailing in certain classes of American society. This mock modesty is carried so far that we even find [in] Upham's *Witchcraft*: "One of her larger limbs was fractured in the attempt to rescue her." [Schele de Vere] Some Americans, with a mock-modesty which is notorious, decline to call a leg a *leg;* they call it a *limb* instead. This tendency is the more remarkable when the greater freedom extended to girls and women is borne in mind. . . .

Perhaps such persons think that it is indelicate for women to have legs, and that therefore they are concealed by garments, and should be concealed in speech. [Farmer] "In Canada, a stranger who could not see would find it difficult to discover much about our conformation. He would learn that both sexes had limbs of some sort, but from any information which our language would give he could not tell whether their limbs were used to stand on or hold by."
—A. C. Geikie, in the *Canadian Journal*, 1857. [Bartlett]

linguister

A talker. Lake Ostego, New York. [Palmer] *Linkister* is the common pronunciation of a New England cant term *linguister*, which the Yankees employ to designate . . . all who possess the "gift of gab" in a special degree. [Schele de Vere]

little end of the horn

An expression . . . said when a ridiculously small effect has been produced after great effort and much boasting. It would be more correct to define it as failing or coming to loss, grief, or poverty in any way. Probably derived from old drinking customs. He who missed at guessing riddles was obliged to drink from the little end or tip of the horn, while the victim drank from the brim. The horn seems in popular parlance to be connected with evil, contrary to old folklore, which made it a symbol of abundance and a protection against evil. [Barrère]

little-lander

An owner of a small acreage. California. [Warnock]

live dictionary

A schoolteacher; a talkative woman. West. [C. Adams]

lobbygow

A pal, in a bad sense. [Tucker]

Lobster Alley

The theatrical section of New York City. [Berrey]

locomote

To walk. [Farmer & Henley]

long-bit

A defaced twenty-cent piece. [Matsell] Fifteen cents. Western U.S. [Farmer & Henley] *Short-bit,* ten cents. [Whitney]

long chalk

"You can't do that by a *long chalk*" is a common expression for a man's inability to accomplish his purpose, derived from the chalk marks of credit on the owner's door or shutter. It is thus often literally applied to the fact that a spectator, for instance, cannot succeed by a *long chalk;* in other words, by all the credit he is able to command. The phrase is one of the oldest in the English language, from the familiarity of people with inns and their customs. [Schele de Vere]

long-fingered

Light-fingered; an epithet for a thief. Montana. [Hayden]

long-handled underwear

Warm underwear having ankle-length legs and usually long sleeves. Canada. [Scargill]

long nine

A cheap cigar. "The long, dank American cigar, nine inches long and nine for a cent." —*Knickerbocker* magazine, December 1847. [Thornton]

long sauce, short sauce

The vernacular of the New England states has preserved the old English usage in speaking of vegetables as "sauce." *Long sauce* is the name applied to parsnips, carrots, and such [lengthier] vegetables, while roots like turnips, onions, etc. are called *short sauce*. [Farmer] Applied humorously to any collection of miscellaneous articles. [Thornton] The legend indeed might have gone further than *long, short*, and *round sauce*, except for the fact that these terms exhaust all the geometrical forms of the vegetable world. [Krapp]

long-sparred

A person with long limbs. Nantucket. [Macy]

long sugar

Molasses. [Thornton] *Long sweetness*, molasses . . . as opposed to sugar, which is *short sweetness*. Newfoundland. [Story]

look at your saddle

A humorous invitation to stop and gossip. Southeastern Missouri. [Crumb]

Lord's supper

The prison fare of bread and water served the men in solitary confinement. [Irwin]

love-hole

A gully or ditch across the road. In the horse-and-buggy days such a depression was supposed to throw lovers into each other's arms. Ozarks. [Randolph & Wilson] *Excuse-me-ma'am*, a bump in the road. West. [R. Adams] *Thank-you-ma'am*, a hollow or ridge in a road which causes persons passing over it in a vehicle to nod the head involuntarily. A New England expression. [Thornton] *Yes-ma'am*, a place where the snow has been worn out in a woods road in winter, causing problems for horse-sleds traveling over it because the road dips too quickly in such places. Newfoundland. [Story]

lubritory

A gas station. [Berrey]

lumberers

Sellers of timber. [Pickering]

lump off

To guess; to make an approximation as to quantity, size, value, etc. "We didn't measure the field but just *lumped* it *off*." Kansas, New York. [Ruppenthal]

lying around loose

An Americanism for being out of a [work] situation, lounging about the town. [Johnson]

The vulgar in America speak much better than the vulgar in Great Britain for a very obvious reason, that being much more unsettled, and moving frequently from place to place they are not so liable to local peculiarities, either in accent or phraseology. There is a greater difference in dialect between one county and another in Britain than there is between one state and another in America.

—John Witherspoon, Scottish-born theologian, president of Princeton, signatory of the Declaration of Independence, and coiner of the term *Americanism,* writing in 1784 in what would become *The Works of Rev. John Witherspoon* (1802)

mahoganize

To paint in imitation of mahogany. [Worcester]

maidenland

When the dower of a wife takes the form of land, the right to which reverts to her family at [her] death, it receives the name of *maidenland.* A Virginian usage. [Farmer]

Maineac

A native of Maine. [Maxfield] *Californiac,* a California enthusiast. [Berrey] *Washingtoniac,* "Every condition of good health happiness, and prosperity is enjoyed to its fullest capacity by *Washingtoniacs.*" —Port Angeles

Tribune-Times. [Lehman] *Buffalonian*, an inhabitant of Buffalo, New York. . . . *Connecticutensian*, an inhabitant of Connecticut. [Craigie]

make a long arm

To reach far, especially when trying to help oneself to food. Kansas. [Ruppenthal] "*Make long arms*, everybody!" Maine, northern New Hampshire. [England]

make the riffle

To overcome all obstacles. Eastern Alabama. [Payne] From the gold-miner's expression describing the collecting of gold dust and small nuggets caught in the *riffles*, or small cleats fastened across the bottom of a slide, down which the powdered rock is carried in a stream of water, the lighter dirt running away with the water and the heavier metal sinking to the bottom. [Irwin]

malahack

To cut up hastily or awkwardly. [Lowell]

mammoxed

A doubtful word, current in the South and West. It seems to bear a meaning of serious personal injury and may, perhaps, be compared with *flummuxed* in the sense of great mental perturbation. [Farmer]

marabou

A term used to describe the child of a . . . mulatto and a negro . . . sometimes applied to the child of a mulatto and an Indian; a person with five-eighths negro blood. Mississippi Valley. [McDermott] Experts profess to be able to distinguish the various grades of color resulting from the admixture of the two races. [Farmer]

marooning

The negro has given us the verb *to maroon*, from *maroon*, the name applied in the West Indies to runaway negroes who live as outlaws in remote and inaccessible parts of the country. The term is used in the Southern States, though now less frequently than formerly, to designate a picnic or excursion party extending over several days. A few families agree thus to go *marooning;* they take tents and cooking utensils, and spend their time away from the haunts of men, and more or less in Robinson Crusoe style. [Schele de Vere] *Marooning* is very similar to what is known in England as "camping out." [Farmer]

marronquin

A large mosquito. Louisiana. [Routh]

Mary Ann

Vile, low, mean, as "That is a *Mary Ann* saloon." *Queen Ann,* beautiful; opposite of *Mary Ann.* Southeastern Ohio. [Parry]

Maryland end

A curious name given to the hock end of a ham, the thick part being called the "Virginia end." These colloquialisms are current in both the states concerned, and are thought by some to allude to a supposed rough resemblance between the contour of these states and a ham. [Farmer]

marywalkers

Trousers worn by women. [Tucker] Derived from Dr. Mary Walker adopting as part of her dress a modified form of this article of male attire. [Farmer]

mast-fed

Used figuratively, meaning irregularly educated; used in the phrase *mast-fed lawyer,* as analogous to *mast-fed swine,* who fed on the acorns they happened to find. Western Indiana. [Brown]

maul and wedges

Maul and wedges, the woodchopper's tools, are often

used to denote the whole of a man's possessions—his movables. "He went across-lots, *maul and wedges,* and we never seen nor hearn of him since." [Schele de Vere]

meeting-seed

Fennel, caraway, dill, or other aromatic and pungent seeds, eaten to prevent drowsiness in church. New England. [Whitney]

meet-market

A corner, drugstore, or other convenient place for meeting; especially such places at the transfer points of [street] car lines. Common but ephemeral. Spokane, Washington. [Lehman]

melon français

A watermelon. Mississippi Valley. [McDermott]

mending hand

On the mending hand, convalescent. A common New England phrase. [Allen]

Methodist feet

A common saying which referred to a person who couldn't dance was "He's got *Methodist feet.*" Newfoundland. [Story]

Mets

In sporting circles, the members of the Metropolitan or New York baseball club are called *Mets.* The term is extending so that probably ere long a New Yorker will be generally be known as a *Met.* [Barrère]

Mexican mustang linament

An early name (about 1854) under which petroleum was sold for medicinal purposes. [Northup]

mezzobrow

A person of medium or average intelligence. [Weseen]

middlings

Flies which buzz around the middle of a shanty [and] won't light where they can be swatted. Pacific Northwest. [McCulloch]

mincy

Fastidious in eating. North Carolina. [Kephart]

misery

For pain; as in "*misery* of the head." Georgia. [Sherwood]

miskubobble

Mistake; error. "The printers made a *miskubobble* in your name." Nebraska. [Pound]

missionate

To perform the services of a missionary. [Pickering]

mission stiff

A tramp who makes it his business to be redeemed in order to obtain food and lodging at mission or rescue society shelters. He is looked down on through trampdom as one who has no pride or ability, although during unusually hard winters or in times of great financial depression many tramps are only too glad to avail themselves of such aid as missions offer them. [Irwin] *Jesus-stiff,* a tramp who specializes in living off missions, the clergy, etc. [Goldin]

Mississippi marbles

Dice. [Berrey]

miss the figure

To err. "Professors Mitchell and Olmstead have *missed the figure* . . . in their speculations on the gold mines." North Carolina. [Eliason]

mistress

The formal pronunciation of *Mrs.* In ordinary conversa-

tion the Ozarker says *Mis'* or *Miz,* but on ceremonious occasions he pronounces *Mistress* very distinctly. The word
is never used in a disparaging sense. [Randolph] *Miss* is
used for married ladies instead of *Mrs.* Rhode Island.
[Ellis]

mitten money

Any kind of a tip, and sometimes a bribe. The term comes
from an extra charge added to a regular pilot's fee during
the winter months when added difficulties of navigation
and the hardships of the season make it seem only fair.
Maine. [Gould]

mizzy

A Louisiana negro expression for a stomach ache.
[Farmer]

moccasin telegram

The spreading of news by word of mouth, originally by
Indian runner. "Word of the white woman ran before the
advancing traders by *moccasin telegram.*" —Agnes Laut's
The Conquest of the Great Northwest, 1908. [Scargill]

mockbeggar

A house that looks well but gives no hospitality. Newfoundland. [Devine]

mollygausauger

A stout fellow. Kentucky. [Dunglison]

mommicks

Momicks is, in Pennsylvania, the curious slang term for a
bad [meat] carver. It arose, in all probability, from a sug-
gestion that such a person was apt to *mommox* the joints
placed before him. [Schele de Vere]

monkey catcher

Amongst the Jamaican negroes this signifies a cute,
shrewd, and level-headed individual . . . who adds a spice

of cunningness to his cleverness. If a piece of work, or any matter, requires special care and attention in its execution, they say, "Soffly *catch monkey,*" meaning take care, exercise tact, don't go blundering—that matter requires finesse and judgment. The phrase is a curious . . . example of the hold which the memory of African life still retains upon them inasmuch as there are no monkeys indigenous to Jamaica. [Barrère]

moonglade

A beautiful word for the track of moonlight on the water. [Lowell] *Moonglade* . . . has come down to seafaring folk from the days of the pilgrim fathers. . . . The so-called Old Colony people, retaining jealously much of the speech of their forefathers, still employ th[is] to embody in language the falling of light aslant hillside or glen by night and by day, and sometimes the track of light leading apparently from the observer to sun or moon is also called thus. [Schele de Vere]

moondown

The setting, or time of setting, of the moon. [Bartlett]

moose-face

A rich, ugly-faced man. A poor but handsome young girl who marries an old, wrinkle-faced, ill-looking rich man is said to have married a *moose-face*. [Matsell]

moose-yard

During the winter the moose, in families of fifteen or twenty, seek the depth of the forest for shelter and food. Such a herd will range throughout an extent of about five hundred acres. . . . The Indians name parts of the forest thus occupied *moose-yards*. [Bartlett]

mopboard

The wash-board which extends around the floor at the

base of the walls in the interior of a house is so called in
New England. [Bartlett]

mops and brooms

Out of sorts. "Since I had the flu I just feel all *mops and
brooms*." Newfoundland. [Story]

mops and brooms

Moses boat

A *Moses boat* is one built of a sufficient capacity to take
from the beach and ship a single hogshead of sugar, used
in the West Indies in places without the convenience of a
wharf. Moses Lowell was a famous boatbuilder at Salis-
bury, Massachusetts, and these boats were apparently
called after him. [Thornton]

mossback

A conservative; one opposed to progress. An old-time pioneer who is satisfied with life and whose narrow ways
prevent development. Used especially in Oregon. [Har-
vey]

mother-spots

Congenital spots on the skin. [Colange]

mountain mutton

Deer killed out of season. New Hampshire. [Clapin]

mouth-bet

When a man in gambling gives only a verbal promise to pay, it is called a *mouth-bet*. [Barrère]

mouthprints

Spoken words, especially when used as evidence. [Weseen]

mud-clerk

The second clerk of a river steamer. So called because it is his duty to go on shore—often at a mere mud bank—to receive or deposit freight. Not facetious. Southeastern Missouri. [Crumb]

muggle-party

An informal social gathering at which *muggle* (a drink made of instantaneous cocoa) is brewed and drunk. Bryn Mawr College. [Savage]

mummock

An Americanism for handle, disarrange, or play with. The word is really obsolete provincial English for *maul*. "Don't *mummock* things about." [Johnson]

mung

Mung, the old preterite of the old English verb to *ming* (from which our modern *mingle*) seems to have been brought to this country, with many kindred forms, by the earliest settlers, and has been preserved here in its purity and power. *Mung news* means confused news; statements which seem contradictory are, in like manner, called *mung*. The original meaning of *mingling* is retained in the Scottish noun *mung,* which means a porridge of two different kinds of meal. [Schele de Vere]

murphies

Potatoes, the chief article of consumption among the

Irish peasantry. The term is current also in America. [Johnson]

mush and molasses

Language indicating a weak intellect or a flabby character. "He talked *mush and molasses*." Northwest Arkansas. [Carr]

mustard shine

An application of mustard to the shoes for the purpose of throwing bloodhounds off the scent. Many prisons and rural constables keep bloodhounds for the purpose of running down criminals. A little mustard oil, olive oil, and mustard, or failing that, simply water and mustard, or any strong spice—even pepper—if applied after the trail has been scented, will render the most melodramatic bloodhound powerless. Prisoners will scrape and save bits of pepper and condiment from their food for this purpose when contemplating an escape. [Kane] The sharp odor of the oil of mustard effectually covers any scent and no doubt actually hurts the delicate nose of the dog. [Irwin]

Though the schoolmaster has long exercised his vocation in these states, the fruit of his labors is but little apparent in the language of his pupils. The amount of bad grammar in circulation is very great; that of barbarism enormous. Of course I do not now speak of the operative [working] class, whose massacre of their mother tongue, however inhuman, could excite no astonishment; but I allude to the great body of lawyers and traders, the men who crowd the exchanges and the hotels, who are heard speaking in the courts and are selected by their fellow-officials to fill high and responsible offices.

—English army captain Thomas Hamilton's
Men and Manners in America (1833)

nagrams

Blues; depression. "I have the *nagrams*." Nebraska. [Pound]

nail-driver

A rapid horse. [Thornton]

nail-sick

Unable to hold nails firmly; said of a much-nailed board. Eastern Massachusetts, Cape Cod. [Wentworth] Leaky at the nail-holes. So, a wooded ship, the bolts and spikes of which are corroded, is said to be *iron-sick*. [Thornton]

naked possessor

Naked possessor is the odd title by which, in Texas and the Southwestern states, the occupant of a farm is known who can show no title to his land. [Schele de Vere]

Nantucket sleigh-ride

The term was made famous by the Nantucket islanders who, in the first part of the nineteenth century, made fortunes from whales. . . . The whale might . . . run for it, in which case the harpooner would let out all the line . . . and let the whale tow the boat at a wild speed until he was tired out. Sometimes the boat caught a wave and foundered, or took aboard so much water that the line had to be cut, but generally the *Nantucket sleigh ride* ended when the whale wore himself out many miles from the ship. [Haywood]

near as peas

Very near. "I come *near as peas* to hurtin' myself." [Hanford]

neck-bang

The short hair of a woman's neck where the line of hair growth begins. [Thornton]

New England of the West

The state of Minnesota; many New Englanders have settled within its borders. [Farmer]

New Hampshire screwdriver

A carpenter's hammer. The inference is that Maine carpenters take the time to set screws right with the proper tool, whereas in New Hampshire the less careful and less skilled workmen just whack 'em home. "New Hampshire" is changed to New York, Massachusetts, New Brunswick, etc. as the occasion requires. [Gould]

newing

Between the new moon and the full; the waxing of the

moon. "Never cut wood when the moon is *newing*." *Losing of the moon,* the period of waning. Newfoundland. [Story]

newity

A novelty; a new experience. Lake Ostego, New York. [Palmer]

news-butcher

A vendor of newspapers and books on a railway train. "The professors were much amused at a sally from the *news-butcher*." Northwest Arkansas. [Carr]

new teeth

False teeth. Kentucky. [Combs]

next grass

In these phrases, *grass* means spring: "seven years old at the *next grass*"; "six years old, *last grass*." [Thornton]

nickel nurser

A stingy individual, one who nurses his funds. [Irwin] *Nickel-pincher,* a stingy person. [Kane]

nip and twitch

To walk with short mincing steps. Central Connecticut. [Mead]

nixes

Nixes is a term used in the railway mail service to denote a matter of domestic origin, chiefly of the first and second class, which is unmailable because addressed to places which are not post offices, or to states etc. in which there is no such post office as that indicated in the address. — *U.S. Post Office Guide,* 1885. [Whitney]

no lager beer

"To think *no lager beer* of oneself," to be self-opinionated—a mere variant of the English slang "to think no small beer." [Farmer]

noon mark

A stake so placed as to mark the edge of a shadow cast by a cabin at noon. The clock, if there is one, is set according to the *noon mark*. Maine. [Maxfield]

noveletic

In a manner peculiar to novels. [Farmer]

number seven steak

So called from the shape of the bone. New Orleans. [Riedel]

Look at the process of deterioration which our Queen's English has undergone at the hands of the Americans. Look at those phrases which so amuse us in their speech and books, at their reckless exaggeration and contempt for congruity, and then compare the character and the history of the nation—its blunted sense of moral obligation and duty to man, its open disregard of conventional right where aggrandizement is to be obtained.

—*Plea for the Queen's English* (1863) by
Reverend Henry Alford, Dean of Canterbury

ocky

A polite word for excrement; a child's term for the excrement of humans or animals. Newfoundland. [Story]

offsprings

Children; used seriously. Southern Pennsylvania. [Wentworth]

oil of joy

Strong drink. Pacific Northwest. [Garrett]

oil-smeller

A new class of people has sprung into existence under the cognomen of *oil-smellers*, who profess to be able to ascertain the proper spot for boring [wells] by smelling the earth. [Bone]

Oklahoma rain

A sand storm, common in that state. [Combs]

old-field

Land formerly in cultivation but now abandoned. North-west Arkansas. [Carr] It has been very common to culti-vate land without fertilizing until exhausted, and then abandon[ing] it, clearing new ground in its stead. Many parts of the South abound in *old-fields*. Southeastern Missouri. [Crumb]

Old Town turkey

The Nantucketer's name for any resident of Martha's Vineyard; from the town of Edgartown, which was for-merly known as Old Town. [Macy]

Omahog

Inhabitant of Omaha, Nebraska. [Berrey]

oncer

He who, or that which, does a thing but once, especially a church member who attends service but once on Sunday. Kansas. [Ruppenthal]

one-brain

A term of disparagement, built on *one-cylinder*. "That fellow is a *one-brain*." Nebraska. [Pound]

one-horse crop

A small crop. It is not uncommon for a poor man to do all his plowing with one horse or mule. He is sometimes called—and often calls himself—a *one-horse farmer*. Southeastern Missouri. [Crumb] *One-horse bank, one-horse insurance company,* [and] *one-horse candidate* are deprecatory epithets. [Barrère]

one o'clock

A secret code word warning that a fly is unbuttoned; also *two o'clock,* should two buttons be unbuttoned. Kansas,

Pennsylvania, Massachusetts, Michigan. [Ruppenthal]

one-poster

A bed built into the corner of a cabin in such a way that only one post is necessary. Ozarks. [Randolph & Wilson]

one's hash

One's business. The phrase may have been invented in America and have been learned by the English in the War of 1812. [Thornton]

on his muscle

"The fellow travels *on his muscle,*" he [relies] on his ability to fight. [Matsell] To travel *on one's shape* is to get on, pay debts, live, or succeed by the virtue of prepossessing looks. [Barrère]

on the bicycle

Running away from blows. Boxing slang. [Weseen]

on the bicycle

on the coast

Near; close at hand. A nautical expression in common use in Nantucket. [Bartlett]

on the grunt

Slightly indisposed; inclined to complain. Snake County, Missouri. [Taylor]

on the half-shell

A very peculiar phrase derived from an oyster thus served. It is applied to anything prepared and ready for use. [Barrère]

on the hummer

Going to the bad. New Orleans. [Routh]

on the prairie

The Indian term for a free gift. "In opening a trade [negotiation] a quantity of liquor is first given *on the prairie,* as the Indians express it in words, or by signs in rubbing the palm of one hand quickly across the other, holding both flat." [Ruxton]

on the rack

Constantly moving about, travelling. "Always *on the rack*" is synonymous with always on the move. *Rack* is an abbreviation of *racket,* a Canadian snowshoe. [Barrère]

on the stocks

In the process of completion. *On the hooks* has much the same meaning. Nantucket. [Macy]

on toast

In America, a very common phrase for anything nicely served. [Barrère]

on wires

Nervous. "Your servants are . . . *on wires* about the alarm." North Carolina. [Eliason]

oodlins

A large quantity. Tennessee. [Whitney]

opera house

Theatre. The word *theatre* is not much used. It connotes debauchery and religious infidelity. Northwest Arkansas. [Carr]

oughtness

From *ought,* to be necessary; a creation of Rev. Joseph

Cook, who defines the office of conscience to be "the determination of rightness and *oughtness* in human affairs." [Farmer]

out of soap

Broke. "Roberts is . . . pretty near *out of soap*." North Carolina. [Eliason]

out on the carpet

In society to find a wife. "That old widower is *out on the carpet*." Northwest Arkansas. [Carr]

outside lots

A term used in the real estate business to indicate lots beyond the city limits. Western Canada. [Sandilands]

overland trout

Bacon [among] American cowboys. [Barrère] *Block Island turkey,* salted cod-fish; Connecticut and Rhode Island. *Digby chicken,* a herring smoked and dried in a peculiar fashion. [Farmer & Henley]

owl car

A street-car running after midnight. Louisiana. [Rontt] *Owl-line, owl-train,* one running very late at night. New York, New Jersey. [Thornton]

owlers

Smugglers. [Matsell]

The general execution of this work is poor. . . . . The mere perusal of his Preface is sufficient to show that he is but slenderly qualified for the undertaking. There is everywhere a great parade of erudition and a great lack of real knowledge; . . . we do not recollect to have ever witnessed . . . a greater number of crudities and errors, or more pains taken to so little purpose.

—Scotland's *Quarterly Review,* commenting on
Noah Webster and his landmark *American Dictionary of
the English Language* shortly after its publication in 1828

pack-off

To blame. "He *packed* it *off* on me." Eastern Kentucky. [Shearin]

pack-water

One who is at one's beck and call; one who will do drudgery for small favors or favorable opinions. "I ain't your *pack-water.*" Southern Illinois. [Rice]

pack-water

palling in

A connection formed by a male and a female thief to steal and sleep together. [Matsell]

pantod

A violent pain; a mild discomfort corresponding to a "conniption fit." [Monroe] The colic, or a similar disorder. Tompkins County, New York. [Cornell]

paragraphist

A newspaper hack. [Thornton]

paresseu

A name given to a lazy, non-cooperating male beaver who is driven from the lodge by the workers. Mississippi Valley. [McDermott]

Paris of America

Cincinnati. This city is also called Queen City and Porkopolis, the latter because of its being a large centre of the pork-packing industry. [Farmer]

park the biscuit

To sit down. *In the biscuit,* in the buttocks. ["One mistake] and you get it *in the biscuit." Hot in the biscuit,* greatly excited; sexually stimulated. [Goldin]

passing-on party

A reception where guests are conducted along a receiving line. Kansas. [Ruppenthal]

pass the 44's

Pass the beans. Loggers graded beans according to [bullet] size, as 22's, 30-30's, 44's, etc. Pacific Northwest. [McCulloch]

patgoe

Patgoes are a kind of invitation to a dance. A wooden bird is fixed on a pole, and carried through the city by some slave. On presenting it to the ladies, they make an offering

of a piece of riband of any length or colour. This is fixed
to the bird, which thus becomes decked with an abundant
and gaudy plumage. A time and place is then set apart for
the fair patrons of the patgoe to assemble, who are usually
attended by their beaux. The patgoe is shot at, and the
fortunate marksman who first succeeds in killing it is pro-
claimed "king." [Williams]

path-walloper

A girl or woman who is seen frequently walking along the
roads or streets with different "followers," or on the lookout for them. Newfoundland. [Story]

paw-pawer

An outlaw; a fugitive from justice. Ozarks. [Randolph]
Paw-paws are equivalent to *bushwhackers,* current in
Missouri. The *paw-paw* is a wild fruit of the genus *Asim-
ina,* on which the bushwhackers are supposed to exist.
[Norton]

pear

To haunt. For *appear;* pronounced as *peer.* A jealous wife
might threaten her husband, "If you marry again, I'll *pear*
to you." Cape Cod. [Chase]

pegging

Mr. Lincoln's naive expression, when he was asked
why he did not make an end to the war, [was] that few
knew what a big job it was. But with his marvelous
cheerfulness and implicit trust in the nation [he]
added, "If we just keep *pegging* away it'll all turn out
right." The term may possibly be taken from the shoemaker's patient work, but to *peg* means at the same
time to strike, and Mr. Halliwell quotes: "I gave him
such a *pegging,*" meaning such a beating. [Schele de
Vere]

penitentiary highball

A mixture of strained shellac and milk. The shellac is run through cheesecloth or through the pithy part of a loaf of bread; the denatured alcohol is thus almost freed of gums and resins. [Goldin]

Peter Rugg

"He'll get home as soon as *Peter Rugg*. He brings weather like *Peter Rugg*." The writer has often heard these and similar sayings in his youth in Massachusetts. They are founded on the following legend: About the end of the seventeenth century, one Peter Rugg and his daughter left Roxbury in a chaise to get to their home in Boston. A friend remarked that a storm was coming up which would prevent his getting home, to which Rugg replied, "I will get home tonight or may I never get home." For a hundred years, whenever a storm was coming, it was always preceded by Peter Rugg in his old chaise, asking the way to his house. He was always in great distress, seeming to be bewildered. One day, when his house had just been sold by auction and had passed into the hands of a stranger, Rugg drove up and then disappeared. His penance was at an end. [Barrère]

pettibockers

A loose garment for girls worn under skirts; contamination of *petticoat* and *knickerbockers*. Kansas. [Ruppenthal]

petticoat trousers

Trousers, very short but with a great width, worn by fishermen. Massachusetts. [Bartlett]

pew-tax

A compulsory [church tax] which used to be levied in New England. [Thornton]

pickaninny

Generally applied to a negro or mulatto infant in the

Southern states. Negroes also apply the same term to white children. [Bartlett] From the Spanish words *pequeño* and *niño*, small. [Schele de Vere]

pick-fiddle

A guitar. Ozarks. [Randolph & Wilson]

pick-up dinner

A *pick-up dinner* is made of such fragments of cold meat, etc. as remain from former meals. Central Connecticut. [Mead] Also called simply a *pick up*. The word is common in the northern states. [Bartlett]

pie-biter

A horse which secretly forages the camp kitchen to indulge his acquired tastes. West. [R. Adams]

pigeon joint

A hardware store where the implements of burglary can be purchased. [Kane] Perhaps from the old cant word *pigeon*, as indicating either a special class of sharper or, more generally, a dupe, although the word is never used in the latter of the two senses in modern criminal argot. [Irwin]

pigs in clover

An emblem of contentment. [Thornton] *On a pig's back*, as one wants to be; all hunky dory; on "easy street." Newfoundland. [England]

pig's whistle

"I'll do it in a *pig's whistle*," that is, in less than no time. [Bartlett] As there exists an Old English equivalent for this in "less than a pig's whisper," and as there is a well known old tavern sign called the *Pig and Whistle*, it is easy to see how one term might be derived from the other. It seems to be a fact, and not a mere philological guess, that "pig and whistle" was originally *pigen wœshœl*, Hail to the Virgin, an amusing instance of bathos. [Barrère]

pile on the agony

To pile on the agony, to intensify a statement or relation by exaggerated or bloodcurdling details. Newspapers *pile on the agony* when writing up murder, divorce, and other sensations. [Farmer]

pineries

In the North and Northwest, the superb tracts of noble woodland which furnish the finest timber in the country are called *pineries*. [Schele de Vere]

pine straw

Dead pine needles. [Weseen]

pint of cider

A small amount, as in the expression "taint as big as a *pint of cider*." Central New York. [White]

pious as a house cat

Pretendedly pious. Maine. [Hanford]

pirooting

Romping like children; going about aimlessly. Louisiana. [Rontt]

pistereen

A [Spanish] coin, formerly current, of the value of one-fifth of a dollar. As they depreciated rapidly, the term *pistareen*, like *picayune*, became synonymous with small or mean, being used in the same way as *one-horse*. New York City. [Farmer]

pixilated

Daffy; "bewildered in the dark." Marblehead, Massachusetts. [Wentworth]

pizzle-grease

A kind of lard or grease made by boiling the penis of a hog. Eastern Alabama. [Payne]

plain people

A negro term for white folks—a tit-for-tat in connection with the term "colored people," as applied by whites to those of the negro race. [Farmer]

planked

Of meat, especially fish, cooked and served on a piece of plank. "Did you ever eat a *planked* shad?" [Craigie]

planticle

A young plant, or plant in embryo. [Webster]

play a good knife and fork

To eat well. "He isn't very well, but he *plays a good knife and fork*." Western Indiana. [Brown]

play a lone hand

To work, travel, or live alone. To avoid any dependence on others. [Weseen]

playing the advantages

The gamblers on the Mississippi use a very refined phrase for *cheating*—"playing the advantages over him." [Marryat]

play out of the cabbage

In golf, to shoot from an obstructed or disadvantageous position. [Weseen]

play out of the cabbage

play whaley

To upset one's plans completely, do the wrong thing, ruin everything. . . . [From] *whaley,* mischief. "Now you've *played whaley.*" Eastern Alabama. [Payne] To attempt what is beyond one's capabilities. "He thought he knew how to set the ladder but he *played whaley.*" Kansas. [Ruppenthal]

plugged money

Silver money is often treated by rogues who bore pieces out and fill the holes with lead or amalgam. The term is applied to men with mental defects: "He is clever, but there is a *plug* in him." [Barrère]

plug-teaching

Teaching trades and arts in casual or evening lessons. "A good deal of boy and girl labour in America is brought into existence by what is called *plug-teaching.* Telegraphy, typesetting, dress-cutting, and designing are among the businesses thus taught, and as a rule the teaching is the merest swindle." —*St. James Gazette.* [Barrère]

plug the Dutchman

In smaller printing plants in years past, the men never had enough material with which to work, such as leads, quads, or spaces. . . . When they complained about not having enough materials they were told to *plug the Dutch-man*—that is, make out as best they could with substitutes such as pasteboard, toothpick slivers, tin, or anything they could find. [Tallman]

plumber's degree

Graduation with minimal effort. Candidates for this degree select "pipe courses." [Weseen]

plunkus

A mythical creature of Maine woodsmen's lore, thus described in the *Bangor Commercial*: "The *plunkus* is about as large as a six months' old hog, and its body is shaped considerably like that of a dog. The head resembles that of an otter, and it has wicked-looking teeth. The most important item in the make-up of a plunkus, however, is the tail. This appendage is about six feet long, and as thick through as a man's arm. At the end of the tail is a large lump of boney gristle as large as an ordinary football. This is the plunkus' chief weapon of defence. The ball of gristle is as hard as gutta percha, and when wielded with all the strength of the powerful tail is a dangerous weapon. Formerly called a *ding-maul*." [Thornton]

pocket-peddler

A person who carries about bottles of distilled liquor for illicit selling. Aroostook County, Maine. [Carr]

poke borak

Applied in colonial conversation to the operations of a person who pours fictitious information into the ears of a credulous listener. [Farmer & Henley]

pokeloken

An Indian word used by hunters and lumbermen in Maine and New Brunswick to denote a marshy place or stagnant pool extending into the land from a stream or pool. [Bartlett]

pollyfox

To quibble or equivocate. "Judge Stewart calls the lawyers down when they *pollyfox* in a case." Kansas. [Ruppenthal]

polt

Polt, a blow, and *polter,* are still quite often heard in the South, and lead us back to the days of the first English settlers in Virginia, who brought the words from their distant home and bequeathed them to their descendants. In England both words are obsolete. [Schele de Vere]

ponny

A sleigh-ride. "Come on out and have a *ponny.*" Long Island. [Wentworth]

poor Foddy's share

A small mess left over from a meal, not enough to serve again. Cape Cod. [Chase]

poor mouth

To make a poor mouth, to plead or pretend poverty. [Thornton]

poot the rug

To die. Pappy's just about ready to *poot the rug.*" Ozarks. [Randolph & Wilson] *Pooter,* to depart speedily. Eastern Maine. [Carr]

pop-crackers

Firecrackers. North Carolina. [Kephart]

porch warmer

A boy who visits a girl and does not offer to take her out to some form of entertainment. [Weseen] *Flat-wheeler,* a young man whose idea of entertaining a girl is to take her for a walk. Bryn Mawr College. [Savage]

portage

A carrying place by the banks of rivers, round waterfalls or rapids. [Pickering] This word has been adopted by geographers, and is universal throughout North America. The Portage Railroad in Pennsylvania is a line over the Alleghany Mountains connecting two lines of canal. [Bartlett]

potato grounds

[Leavening] yeast made from potatoes. Newfoundland. [Story]

potty-baker

A potter. This Dutch word *pottebakker* is still common in New York. Potter's clay is there called *potty-baker's clay*. [Bartlett]

potwalloper

A man in England who occupies a house, no matter how small, and boils a pot in it, thus qualifying himself for voting. . . . The American meaning is connected with the use of *wallop,* in the sense of beating, striking. The figure is apparently taken from the manner in which such an unfortunate being would be apt to knock the kitchen pots about. In Pennsylvania, *pot-wrestler* is occasionally used for the same purpose. [Schele de Vere]

pound of wool

"No bigger than a *pound of wool,*" not very large. Southwestern Wisconsin. [Savage]

pound-party

An assemblage, usually the parishioners of a country clergyman whose salary is inadequate to his support, which on an evening agreed upon meets at his house carrying tea, coffee, and other articles of necessity put up in pound packages as contributions to him. . . . *Donation party,* a party consisting of the friends and parishioners of a country clergyman assembled together, each individual bringing some article of food or clothing as a present to him. [Bartlett]

prairie comedian

An inferior actor. Theater slang. [Weseen]

prairie oyster

A raw egg swallowed whole, or drunk in vinegar, brandy, etc. Canada. [Scargill]

prairie strawberries

A slang name for beans. [R. Adams] *Mexican strawber-*

ries, red Mexican beans. . . . *Pilgrim marbles,* Boston-baked beans. [Berrey] *Lumberjack strawberries,* prunes. Pacific Northwest. [McCulloch]

prairillion

A small prairie, or meadow. Mississippi Valley. [McDermott]

prayer-handles

Knees. Maine, northern New Hampshire. [England] *Prayer-bones,* the knees. [Farmer]

preacher's dinner

A term used among the Pennsylvania Dutch to mean a sumptuous meal. Special occasions such as a baptism or a marriage would be accompanied by a bounteous dinner, as would any visit by the minister. [Tallman]

prick down

To track down; to look for. "These six men to be *pricked down* by ye towns." Providence, Rhode Island. [Ellis]

printery

A printing establishment. [Tucker] Of the same class of words as *bindery, bakery, creamery,* etc. [Farmer] *Bleachery,* a place for bleaching. [Lyons] *Cheesery,* a cheese factory. [Thornton] *Doughnutry,* a light lunch cafe. Berkeley, California. [Lehman] *Dimery,* a ten-cent store. [Weseen] *Drunkery,* a saloon. [Craigie] Double Bridges [Georgia] . . . has three or four houses, with one or two *drunkeries.* [Sherwood] *Breadery,* [a bakery]. Seattle. [Garrett] *Grapery,* a place where grapes are grown. [Lyons]

Protestant whisker

Sideburns and beard under the chin. Newfoundland. [Story]

prunes in the voice

To have *prunes in the voice,* to speak huskily, the cause being emotion. [Farmer]

puckaloon

A foolish man. Newfoundland. [England]

puckersnatch

This term the old-timers used to describe a hasty and unskillful job of sewing. The word, invented by some old lady with a penchant for pungent phrase, describes admirably both the appearance of the completed work on the garment and the motions of the person impatiently and hurriedly plying her needle. New England. [Haywood]

pullikins

A dentist's forceps. This is an interesting example of folk-etymology. *Pelican* is the name of a dentist's forceps, so-called because shaped like a pelican's beak. Naturally *pullikan* resulted, and the final *s* was added on the analogy of *tongs, pincers,* etc. Eastern Alabama. [Payne]

pult

For *pulse*. Some country doctors think *pulse* is plural, and say, "A very good *pult,*" [and] "Your *pulse are* strong." [Bartlett]

pumpkin flood

[A flood] that inundated the valleys of the Susquehanna and its tributaries in the fall of 1787. The cornfields were swept bare, and the yellow pumpkins that thickly dotted the surface of the swollen streams were so conspicuous that the descriptive name . . . survives among the household words in southern New York. [Fox]

pumpkin heads

[Samuel] Peters explains why New Englanders were called *pumpkin heads.* As every male was required to have his hair cut round by a cup, "when cups were not to be had, they substituted the hard shell of a pumpkin, which being put on the head every Saturday, the hair is cut by the shell all round the head." [Krapp]

pumptack

An ordinary carpet-tack, popularly supposed to be so named from its use in fastening the leather valve of a pump; perhaps a corruption for *thumb-tack*. Cape Cod. [Chase]

puncture lady

A woman who prefers to sit on the sidelines at a dance and gossip rather than dance. She usually makes a good job of *puncturing* someone's reputation. West. [R. Adams]

pure quill

A strange synonym for "the real thing," the essence of an argument. Also applied to any object thought worthy of superlative praise. [Farmer]

pussy-gutted

Corpulent. Northwest Arkansas. [Carr]

put sugar in one's ear

To give one a hint. "I'll put a little sugar in your ear." Northwest Arkansas. [Carr]

It is not to Texas, or to California, or to Maine, or indeed to any place in America that we should go to find our "standard English," whether in word, in idiom, or in pronunciation. The language spoken in those places may be a very polite one, very admirable in every respect, but is it not necessarily standard English; and just in so far as it deviates from the language of the most cultivated society in England, it fails to be English.

—American Shakespearean scholar
Richard Grant White's *Everyday English* (1880)

quaker gun

An imitation gun made of wood or other material and placed in the port-hole of a vessel, or the embrasure of a fort, in order to deceive an enemy; so called from its inoffensive character. [Bartlett]

quartee

One-fourth of a "bit," or twelve and a half cents; later, one-fourth of ten cents. Louisiana. [Rontt] *Ninepence,* twelve and a half cents—the old "shilling" of New York. [Tucker]

quattlebums

Boasters; *quattlebummery,* nonsense. [Thornton]

queen's taste

Perfection. "He did it to a *queen's taste*." Northwest Arkansas. [Carr]

quibberdick

A person who always argues. [Weseen]

quibberdick

quiblets

A kind of witticism much in vogue in negro minstrelsy. A man makes a remark which calls forth a question, and the reply involves a jesting equivoque. [Barrère]

quiddle

To busy oneself about trifles. New England. [Dunglison] *Quiddles,* disorder in the head; moping disease in horses; dizziness. [Humphreys]

quint

An abbreviation of *quintessence,* applied to a pernickity old maid; from a local saying describing such a person, "She's the quintessence of old maid, stewed down to a half pint." The corresponding adjective is *quinty.* Nantucket. [Macy]

quituate

A facetious blend of *graduate* and *quit.* "Is he still in school? No, he *quituated.*" Nebraska. [Pound]

quoke

Quaked. Virginia. [Green]

Both the purist and the innovator are necessary factors in the development of a cultured tongue. Without the purist, our language would change with extravagant rapidity. Our vocabulary, for example, would give daily hospitality to hosts of new words which have nothing but whim to justify them, and which would be soon superseded by equally lawless formations. Without the innovator, our language would come to a dead stop, so far as literary expression is concerned, and in a short time the speech of books would have lagged so far behind the speech of conversation that the two would form different dialects.

—Harvard language professors James Greenough and
George Kittredge's *Words and Their Ways in English Speech* (1914)

rackergaited

Loose-jointed. Maine, northern New Hampshire. [England]

rain tadpoles

To rain heavily. Alabama. [Hanford]

raise a bead

This expression is used [in] the West, and means to bring to a head, to make succeed. The figure is taken from brandy, rum, or other liquors, which will not "raise a bead" unless of the proper strength. [Bartlett]

rantum scoot

A term we believe peculiar to Nantucket, and very old. It

means a day's cruise or picnic about the island, usually a drive, but it might be on foot. The distinctive feature of such an excursion is that the party has no definite destination, but rather a roving comission, in which respect such a trip differs from a "squantum." Does this mean to *scoot* at *random*? [Macy]

rathers

Choice; preference. "State your *rathers*." Virginia. [Dingus]

rattage

Loss by rats. [Thornton]

rattage

real Limburger

The *real Limburger* is used grotesquely in many ways, especially [in regards] to anything actually German. Limburger cheese has a strong smell which is intolerable to those who are not accustomed to it. [Barrère]

recollember

A negroism for *recollect* or *remember*. [Bartlett]

redd

To make tidy; used only of the hair. Appalachia. [Dingus] *Redding comb,* a comb with very fine teeth used to clean hair and scalp thoroughly. Nebraska, Texas. [Ruppenthal]

Red up, to make a tidy house. "Wait till I *redden up* a bit." [Maxfield]

redemptioner

One who *redeems* himself by services, or whose services are sold to pay certain expenses. [Dunglison] In the early colony days it was common for vessels coming from England to Virginia to bring redemptioners, who were technically known as "indentured servants" because they were bound to serve a stipulated time to pay, or "redeem" the cost of their transportation. Some of these *redemptioners* were convicts banished to America for crime, but all of them were sold and, for the time being, treated as slaves. [Farmer]

red in the comb

When a mountain man says of a woman that "her comb sure is red," he means that she is in a state of sexual excitement. . . . A fowl with a bright red comb is thought to be healthy and sexually active, while one with a pale comb is in poor condition. Ozarks. [Randolph & Wilson] *Cut [one's] comb,* to humiliate. Virginia. [Green] "It *cut his comb* mightily when she refused his company." Southeastern Missouri. [Crumb]

red shirt

A refractory prisoner. In some prisons a man who has made an attempt at an escape, or who has taken part in a prison mutiny, is forced to wear a bright red shirt. [Kane]

reinikaboo

A newspaper story which is midway between a fake and a statement of fact, yet having a certain origin and shadowy foundation. [Cornell]

reluct

To strive or struggle against; [from] Latin *reluctor, re* and *luc-*

tor, to struggle. [Webster] The use of this verb . . . does not frequently occur in the writings of Americans. [Pickering]

rench

For *rinse.* Georgia. [Sherwood] "*Rench* out your mouth," said a fashionable dentist. [Hotten]

repeater

A person who votes more than once at an election, a custom extensively practised in the cities of New York and Philadelphia. [Bartlett]

rhyme of oaths

A fit of cursing. Newfoundland. [Story]

rib wrenches

A slang name for spurs. West. [R. Adams]

ride and tie

Travel conditions in colonial times were difficult and expensive. As a result, an ingenious device to aid people of limited means developed. One couple would ride a horse a certain distance, tie it to a tree, then go on by foot. A second couple, following them on foot, would finally catch up with the now rested horse and ride it on ahead of the first couple, leaving it for them in turn. Thus, all four did some walking but all got a rest. [Tallman] The two riders ran the risk the horse might be stolen while tied, yet the risk was not great. New England. [Haywood] The saying is often used figuratively to describe a scandalous triangle involving two men and one woman. Ozarks. [Randolph & Wilson]

ride the cushions

To travel first class. Pacific Northwest. [Lehman] *On the cushions,* originally applied to one riding on the cushioned seats of a passenger train, and therefore having money. The phrase has been extended to include any state of comfort, wealth, or ease. [Irwin] *Close to the cushion,* economically. "They always had to live pretty *close to the cushion*." Chicago. [Curtiss] *Against the cushion*, in difficulty. Southeastern Ohio. [Parry]

right croaker

A physician who does business with the underworld, treating wounds without reporting to police. [Goldin]

rimpshions

An abundance. "There's *rimpshions* of squirrels in Hickory Cove." North Carolina. [Kephart]

rippit

A great noise. "He made a great *rippit*." Kentucky. [Fruit]

ripsniptious

Smart, spruce. South and West. [Dunglison]

rising finger, rising hand

An extremity swollen from infection. Newfoundland. [Story]

risk an eye

To be certain of. "I'll *risk an eye* on it." Northwest Arkansas. [Carr]

riverbanking

Taking a walk along the riverbank; used of a walk taken by a boy and girl together. Minnesota. [Klaeber]

road-agent

A highwayman. [Thornton] *Road-agent* is the name applied in the mountains to a ruffian who has given up honest work in the store, in the mine, in the ranch, for the perils and profits of the highway. [Dixon]

rocking-chair money

Unemployment insurance. Western Canada. [Scargill]

roger

The word *roger,* as used by many young people in the Ozarks, is a verb meaning to manage, to control. Taken for a ride in a new car, a lady asked the driver, "Do you think you can *roger* this thing all right?" But among the old-timers *roger* means copulate, particularly among sheep and goats. [Randolph & Wilson]

rolling-roads

So called in Maryland and Virginia from the old custom of rolling tobacco to market in hogsheads. [Bartlett] Their meandering routes were due to the foremen's taking the easiest means of getting to market. Each crate weighed from eight hundred to a thousand pounds. [Tallman]

roorback

A falsehood; a bogus newspaper article, especially a false allegation issued for political purposes, and now a general term for any political forgery or fiction. The word was derived from the fact that in 1844 a Whig newspaper, the *Ithaca Chronicle,* published for political purposes alleged extracts from *The Travels of Baron Roorback* [1836] which were proved almost on their appearance to have been a set-up scheme to deceive the public. [Clapin]

roorback

rooster and ox

[It is] absurd prudishness to shrink from the good old English word *cock,* and translate it into the unmeaning *rooster,* as if it were not known that all birds are roosters, and hens certainly quite as much as cocks. Dr. Hyde Clark, perhaps too severely, calls the term *rooster* "an American ladyism for *cock,*" and a recent English writer professes to have heard a "rooster and ox" [for "cock-and-bull"] story in the United States! [Schele de Vere] *Crower,* a pruddish euphemism for *cock.* [Farmer]

rooster's egg

In Massachusetts, *rooster's egg* is used facetiously for a large egg. [Chase] A small hen's egg. Virginia. [Green]

rotten logging

A term used when romantic couples sit on a log by moon-light to court, a practice seldom followed on the range. West. [R. Adams]

rough dry

Of clothes, dry but not smoothed or ironed. [Craigie]

round dance

Waltz, polka, or schottisch. Southern Illinois. [Rice]

round voyage

One which includes going and returning. [Thornton]

rubber bum

A hobo or panhandler who travels in an old automobile, and is regarded as something of a snob in consequence. [Goldin]

rumbud

A "grog blossom." The popular name of a redness occa-sioned by the detestable practice of excessive drinking. *Rumbuds* usually appear first on the nose, and gradually extend over the face. [Webster]

run emptins

To show signs of not holding out well, as for instance in a speech or other enterprise. Probably from the analogy of a beer-barrel. Western Connecticut. [Babbitt] To *run empty-ings* is where a speaker or a writer continues to speak or write after he has delivered himself of every thing of any consequence. [Bartlett]

run one's face

To *run one's face* is a frequent phrase meaning to obtain money upon credit in return for the borrower's name being placed on the *face* of a promissory note, which is then *run*. [Schele de Vere]

rush the growler

To go or send often for beer to be brought in a *growler,* a pitcher or pail. [Thornton] To bring home beer in a pail or pitcher. [Tucker] Explained by the 1888 *New York Herald* quotation: "One evil of which the inspectors took particular notice was that of the employment by hands in a number of factories of boys and girls under ten and thirteen years to fetch beer for them, in other words to *rush the growler.*" [Farmer]

ruttier

An old traveler acquainted with roads; an old soldier; from *route,* French *routier.* [Webster]

I have been not a little disappointed, and made suspicious my own judgment, on seeing the Edinburgh reviewers, the ablest critics of the age, set their forces against the introduction of new words into the English language. . . . Certainly so great growing a population spread over such an extent of country, with such a variety of climates, of productions, of arts, must enlarge their language to make it answer the purpose of expressing all ideas, the new as well as the old. . . . But whether will these adulterate or enrich the English language? Has the beautiful poetry of Burns, or his Scottish dialect, disfigured it?

—Thomas Jefferson's *Writings,* volume 4

sacred desk

A pulpit. [Thornton]

saddlebag surgeon

In the early days of settlement in the West, a doctor who did his rounds on horseback, carrying his instruments, medicines, etc. Canada. [Scargill]

salt a mine

To put good mineral specimens in a poor mine to deceive purchasers. [Weseen]

salt-water vegetables

In New York, a cant term for oysters and clams. [Bartlett]

same old six and seven

The same old routine, story, etc. Virginia. [Dingus]

sandlot Kearny

A political agitator; from the fact that a man named Kearny used in the 1880s to harangue mass meetings on the outlying sandlots of San Francisco. San Francisco Bay. [Lehman]

sandola

A large freight boat made from a single log. Pennsylvania. [Shoemaker]

sannup

Among the American Indians . . . the husband of a squaw. "Mindful still of *sannup* and of squaw." —Ralph Waldo Emerson's *Musketaquid*, 1847. [Lyons]

savagerous

Like *ruinous*, used in the South to give still greater force to *savage*. [Schele de Vere]

save your gizzard

To use extreme effort. "You can't do that to *save your gizzard*," i.e., no matter how hard you try. Cape Cod. [Chase] *To have sand on one's gizzard*, to have courage. Virginia. [Dungus] *Gizzard*, the seat of one's courage. East Alabama. [Payne] *Sand in one's craw*, courage. "He hasn't any *sand in his craw*." Western Indiana. [Brown]

savior's letter

A letter, usually printed, purported to be by Christ, kept as a moral guide and as a charm. Newfoundland. [Story]

savior's letter

JEFFREY KACIRK

scallyhoot

To be off; to skedaddle. A Texas form. [Farmer]

scandiculous

A blend of *scandalous* and *ridiculous*. Montana. [Hayden]

scatterationist

The expressive but not very euphonious word which somebody has coined to designate those political quibblers who neutralize their force by pursuing their crotchety views upon every minor point and by co-operating with nobody. [Bartlett] Formerly political but now commonly colloquial. [Farmer]

scattery

Hurried; eat-and-run. "Such a *scattery* dinner!" [Atkinson]

scheme school

To *scheme school* means to play truant. Peterboro, Ontario. [Chamberlain]

schoolhousing

Formal education. North Carolina. [Cooper]

scissible

Capable of being cut or divided by a sharp instrument, as *scissible matter.* [Webster]

scoggins

An object of ridicule or tricks. Massachusetts, Florida, Georgia. [Wentworth]

sconick

To hurry about; also *sconick round.* "I could see plain enough which side you was on without *sconickin' round* after you." —John Neal's *The Down Easters,* 1833. [Farmer & Henley]

scoon

Various nautical terms peculiar to America, or taken into English from American sources, came in during the eighteenth century, among them *schooner*. . . . *To scoon* was a verb borrowed by New Englanders from some Scots dialect, and meant to skim or skip over the water like a flat stone. According to a historian of the American merchant marine, the first *schooner* was launched at Gloucester, Massachusetts, in 1713. . . . The earliest recorded example of *schooner* is from Bartlett's fourth edition (1877). [Mencken]

Scotch kiss

A kiss with the cheeks drawn between the jaws (teeth). Kansas. [Ruppenthal]

scratch gravel

Be gone! This expression may be compared with "to pad the hoof" and similar phrases. [Farmer]

scrimshandy

An Americanism signifying the objects in ivory and bone carved by whalemen during their long voyages. Synonymous with *scrimshaw*. [Barrère]

scriptorean

Scripturist. Georgia. [Sherwood]

scrongo

An automobile; Northern California localism. [Lehman]

scroobly

Untidy. "My, but my hair is *scroobly*." Nebraska. [Pound]

scroof

To live with a friend and at his expense. Thieves are in the habit of *scroofing* with an old pal when they first come out of prison, until they can steal something for themselves. [Matsell]

scroop

To creak like new shoes or boots. . . . In the old days, the *scrooping* of new, "Sunday" boots gave great pleasure to the wearers while walking into church. It indicated a degree of prosperity. I heard an old-timer say, "The spring of the big haul of seals, you couldn't hear your ears in church with [all the] *scroopy* boots." Newfoundland. [Devine]

scull-drag

To do a servant's work. Louisiana. [Rontt]

scup

A New York boy's term, little heard, signifying to swing. From the Dutch *schoppen*. [Farmer]

scurryfunge

A hasty tidying of the house between the time you see a neighbor and the time she knocks on the door. This tends to be coastal. The upland version would be to *teakittle up*. Maine. [Gould]

sea-circled

Surrounded by the sea. [Webster]

seam squirrel

A louse or flea. [Weseen] *Pants rabbits, shimmy lizards,* lice. [Berrey]

second-day wedding

A reception given by newly-married couples on their return from the honeymoon. [Farmer]

sectionary

Belonging to a section of a country; local. I have once also met with *sectional* in the same sense. [Pickering]

see black

To suffer the lapses of vision caused by exposure to thirst, heat, and glaring sunlight. Southwest. [Harvey]

seedfolks

Ancestors. Coastal Maine. [Wentworth]

seeing the look

Noting a family resemblance; usually applied in the case

of children to parents or to other ancestors. We speak of *seeing the* "Folger *look*." Nantucket. [Macy]

see monkeys

To be overcome by the heat while working. The heat waves are called "monkeys." When one laborer shows signs of exhaustion, the others say, "Look out, the monkeys are after you." North Carolina. [Steadman]

seenless

Invisible [blind]. "A *seenless* man gets along somehow." [Atkinson]

see the elephant

A slang term taken from wandering menageries in which the elephant generally closes the exhibition as the most attractive feature of the show. Hence the phrase means to have seen all and to know everything. [Schele de Vere] To undergo any disappointment of high-raised expectations. It is in fact nearly or quite synonymous with the ancient phrase "go out for wool and come back shorn." For instance, men who volunteered for the Mexican war, expecting to reap lots of glory and enjoyment but who instead found only sickness, fatigue, privations, and suffering, were said to have *seen the elephant*. Afterwards, those who went to California with golden expectations and returned disappointed were said to have *seen the elephant*. [Bartlett]

seep

Used in New England to signify the process of straining. Coffee is said to be *seeped* when run through clear muslin to clear it. Undrained "wet" land is *seepy*. [Farmer]

seroon

A bale or package. A seroon of almonds is the quantity of two hundred pounds, of anise seed, from three to four hundred weight, of Castile soap, from two hundred and a half to three hundred and three-quarters. [From] Spanish *seron*, a frail or basket. [Webster]

set-along

"When my oldest was a little *set-along* child . . ." North Carolina. [Kephart]

settle one's hash

A picturesque phrase expressive of such manner of acting as will finally silence an opponent. [Schele de Vere]

set up with

To court. "Harvey's been *settin' up with* Jane." Maine, Northern New Hampshire. [England]

seven by nine

Inferior; third rate. The phrase probably originated from the size of common window-glass. "These Indians . . . are now penned up in little *seven-by-nine* reservations up there in the northern part of Wisconsin." [Thornton]

seven hundred dollars

Extraordinarily. "I'm sicker'n *seven hundred dollars*." "It snowed like *seven hundred dollars*." Snake County, Missouri. [Taylor]

seven-shooter

A firearm with seven chambers. [Thornton] The more recent "revolver," now quite common in the West, is the *five-* or *six-shooter*, according to the number of barrels. [Schele de Vere]

shad-belly

A Philadelphia term for a Quaker, in special reference to the dress worn by the [Society of] Friends. The Quaker coat, in its outline from the neck to the end of the skirt, is cut in a curve exactly corresponding to that of the ventral line of a shad. [Barrère]

shadkin

A marriage broker; from Yiddish *shadchen*. . . . He is a very useful man. He finds out spinsters who have money and then he makes a bargain with some fellow who wants a wife with money and gets the couple introduced. Ten percent of the dowry goes to the *shadkin*. [Barrère]

shagpoke-gut

A tremendous eater; from *shagpoke*, a bird which doesn't care what it eats, just so it eats all the time. Pacific Northwest. [McCulloch]

shaker the plate

This expression, meaning to eat everything on your plate, was much used in northern New York State. It came from the practice of the religious community of Shakers of taking no more from the communal pot than could be eaten. [Tallman]

shamocrat

One who pretends to be possessed of wealth, influence, rank, or indeed any quality which is only conspicuous by its absence. [Farmer]

shank of the evening

The early part of the evening. . . . Common in rural New England fifty years ago. [Monroe] The latter part of the evening. Eastern Kentucky. [Shearin]

sharooshed

Taken aback, surprised; disappointed, disgusted. Newfoundland. [Wentworth]

shattered prices

An Americanism for reduced prices. [Johnson]

sheep corner

Sheep are devilishly hard to catch, and a prudent farmer always made a special pen in his pasture corner into which the sheep could be driven for close handling. Anybody "caught in a sheep corner" will be without an answer, perhaps caught in a lie. Maine. [Gould]

shellback

The sailor's commendatory term for the landsman's "old salt." Some authorities say that it comes from his back being bent like a shell. But it seems . . . the implication is that the shellback is growing barnacles from having been at sea so long. The term is fairly well known to landspeople. [Colcord]

shinnicked

Benumbed, paralysed with the cold, especially when accompanied by contraction of the muscles and violent shivering. Newfoundland. [Story]

ship's wife

When a prosperous old-time Maine sea captain set a ne'erdo-well son up in some business, the lad would own his vessel but, having no experience, would require a professional navigator . . . to sail it for him. Such a navigator was the *ship's wife*. The term is still used for an obsequious assistant or a man who does all the work without any credit. [Gould]

shoe-mouth deep

To a depth equal to the height of an ordinary shoe, as in mud or snow. Snake County, Missouri. [Taylor]

shopped

The inmates of a sleeping car at Pittsburgh were turned out by the porter for the reason that it had to be *shopped*—sent to the repair shop. [Farmer]

short ear

A rowdy. *Long-ear,* a sober student, religiously-minded student. American university slang. [Barrère]

short rows

Some strait-laced Ozark folks wriggle a little at any reference to "the short rows." This expression is often used in connection with copulation, and means a brief interval just preceding the orgasm. "We was just gittin' into *the short rows*," said a backwoods philanderer, "when I heerd the front gate slam." The phrase is perhaps derived from plowing in irregular clearings where the last few rows to be plowed are the shortest. Ozarks. [Randolph & Wilson]

shot in the neck

One of the numerous expression for being drunk which abound in the Union. Louisiana. [Schele de Vere]

shotten

A fish that has cast its spawn. "Lean as a *shotten* herring." Cape Cod. [Chase]

shouting bee

An occasion when there is much shouting as a result of religious emotion. [Mathews]

shovelful o' work

Very little work. Maine, northern New Hampshire. [England]

shrieking sisterhood

An opprobrious, journalistic term applied to women who take the lead in matters of reform connected with their sex. [Barrère]

shucks

Something worthless. "Church ain't *shucks* to a circus." —Mark Twain's *Tom Sawyer*. [Ramsay]

sick as a horse

"I'm as *sick as a horse*" is a vulgar phrase which is used when a person is exceedingly sick. As a horse is larger than a man, it is customary to use it by way of comparison to denote largeness or excess either in a serious or ludi-crous way, as *horse-chestnut, horse-leech, horse-laugh,* &c. [Bartlett]

sidehill baby

An illegitimate child. Texas. [Atwood]

silver scale

A silver five-cent piece or three-cent piece; not a "nickel piece." Southwestern Wisconsin. [Savage]

silver thaw

The coating of ice formed on trees in the spring by a frost following quickly on a thaw. Newfoundland. [Devine]

simon-pure

"The real *Simon Pure*" is a phrase meaning the genuine article, the real thing; as, "This whisky is the real *Simon Pure.*" [Bartlett] "An actual *simon-pure* tablecloth." — Mark Twain's *A Connecticut Yankee.* [Ramsay]

sing Indian

To act in a proud or defiant manner. [Craigie]

singlings

The liquor of the first distillation ("low wines") which moonshiners redistill at a lower temperature to make moonshine. North Carolina, Kentucky. [Kephart]

sing small

To have little to say for yourself. [Matsell]

sitting britches

When the old-timers said of anyone, "He has his *sitting britches* on," they referred more to a state of mind than an actual garment. Such a person was one in the mood to take his ease and stay. New England. [Haywood]

sixteen-for-one

Milk; sixteen men for one can of milk. Soldiers' slang. [Weseen]

skeewinkle, skwywise

Twisted. "Her tie's all *skeewinkle*." Nebraska. [Pound]
Skwywise, askew. "This picture hangs skwy[wise]." Salem,
Massachusetts. [Briggs]

skeezix

In use in and around Philadelphia to designate a man not
altogether to be trusted. Used by Bret Harte in the sense of
a shiftless, good-for-nothing fellow, as the title of a story.
[Pickering] Bartlett defines this as a mean, contemptible
fellow. The writer has always understood it to mean a fidgety, fussy little fellow. Both may be right. In Cornwall,
skeese means to frisk about. *Skicer* is "a lamb which kills
itself by excess of activity." [Barrère]

skin your own skunks

This highly expressive phrase is applied to any man when
he is exhorted to do his own dirty or difficult work without involving another in it. [Barrère]

skwuzzy

Term of approbation or compliment. "What a *skwuzzy*
hat!" Nebraska. [Pound]

sky-parlor

An Americanism for an attic. [Johnson]

skyugle

A factitious word varying in orthography, which means
everything, anything, or nothing—a term claiming inser-
tion by right whenever one is at a loss for a word. It is said
to have originated with the Union soldiers during the Civil
War. The *Army and Navy Journal,* 11 July, 1864 [re-
ported]: "A corps staff-officer . . . informed me that he had
been out on a general *skyugle.* He had *skyugled* along the
front when rebels *skyugled* a bullet through his clothes;
that he should *skyugle* his servant who had, by the way,

skyugled three fat chickens; that after he had *skyugled* his dinner he proposed to *skyugle* a nap." [Farmer]

slab-sided, slab-bridged

Both terms . . . are taken from the *slabs,* outside pieces of timber which occasionally serve to make country bridges of peculiarly unstable and unsafe character. [Schele de Vere] Whoever has driven over a stream [on] a bridge made of slabs will feel the picturesque force of the epithet *slab-bridged,* applied to a fellow of shaky character. [Lowell]

slangander

To slander in a silly manner. *Slangoosing,* women's tittle-tattle, backbiting, or gossip. [Barrère]

slantindicular

A word evidently made up from the verb to *slant* and the latter part of the word *perpendicular.* [Schele de Vere] Originally an Americanism, now part of London "high life below stairs." [Hotten]

slatch

A short gleam of fine weather; an interval in a storm. When caught away from home in a heavy rain, we plan, if possible, to wait for a *slatch* before starting to return. The term is also used in the sense of a respite from labor, as "I had a *slatch* in my work." A word still in quite common use on the island among the older people. Nantucket. [Macy]

slathers

A great quantity. "I am going to be a clown at a circus. They get *slathers* of money—most a dollar a day." — Mark Twain's *Tom Sawyer.* [Bartlett]

slaunchways

Slantingly. North Carolina, Illinois, Kansas. [Kephart]

sleep and eat

To provide with lodging and board. "Wages are $45 a month, and you have to *sleep and eat* the man besides." Wyoming. [Bruner]

slewer

A servant girl; a vulgar word only heard among fast young men. [From] *sloor, slure,* Dutch slang [for] a poor, common woman. [Barrère] "They say here [in Philadelphia, that the servant girls] ain't nothing but *slewers,* but I seed sum that I would t[ake] for respectable g[ir]ls if I had seed 'em in Georgia." [Jones]

slice off a cut loaf

Continuation of some wrongful indulgence, especially sexual. Kansas. [Ruppenthal]

slit-spoon

A fork. [Optic]

slumguzzling

Deceiving, humbugging. [Barrère]

slumming party

A party or group that visits the slums or low resorts for charitable purposes, or out of curiosity. "It's a society fad now to have what are called 'slumming parties.' . . . They get detectives to protect them, and then go to the tenements . . . and pry into their privacy and poverty just out of curiosity." [Ford]

smart chance

A good deal, large amount, large company, great number. Georgia. [Sherwood] "Quite a smart chance," or "a right smart chance," means more; and "a mighty smart chance" is the superlative, and means a very large quantity. These singular expressions, used in the Southern and Western States, are never heard in the East. *Smart sprin-*

kle, a good many. Used in the interior of the Western States. [Bartlett] "He lost a right *smart chance* of blood." [Dunglison]

smatchy

Tainted, spoiled; of meat. Newfoundland. [England]

smear-case

A preparation of milk made to be spread on bread, whence its name; otherwise called *cottage cheese.* In New York it is called *pot-cheese.* [Bartlett]

smike

A bit of. "We haven't had a *smike* of rain all summer." Prince Edward County, Ontario. [Chamberlain]

smoked lamp

A blackened eye. Boxing slang. [Weseen]

smoked Scotchman

They married . . . among the Indians, and to this day some of the finest names in Canadian history are perpetuated in Indian tents along the Athabasca and Mackenzie, and their bearers are known as "smoked Scotchmen." [Scargill]

smudge

A smothered fire used to keep off mosquitoes. Aroostook County, Maine. [Carr]

snatchback

A change for the worse; downfall. "That's a *snatchback* for him." Northwest Arkansas. [Carr]

snatch baldheaded

To treat with severity, especially to chastise corporally. "If I ever catch you at that, I'll *snatch* you *baldheaded.* Kansas, New England, New York, the South. [Ruppenthal]

snivver

A good definition would be "immediately after." One says, "I'll be over to your house *snivver* dinner." The presumption is that the speaker means "as soon as I have had my dinner." Nantucket. [Macy]

snollygoster

Exact meaning unknown, but plainly used as a term of disparagement. "We once knew a miserly old *snollygoster*." Nebraska. [Pound]

snowslip

A mass of snow which slips down a mountain's side. [Lyons] *Mountain-slide,* an avalanche. [Thornton]

snucker

"I'll *snucker*" means I'll not do it. Western Pennsylvania. [Hart]

snuff-dipping

A mode of taking tobacco practised by some of the lower class of women in the United States consisting of dipping a brush among snuff and rubbing the teeth and gums with it. [Hunter] A little pine stick or bit of rattan about three inches long, split up like a brush at one end, is first wetted and then dipped into snuff . . . for cleansing the teeth. [Bartlett]

soap-lock

A lock of hair made to lie smooth by soaping it. Hence also a name given to a low set of fellows who lounge about the markets, engine-houses, and wharves of New York, and are always ready to engage in midnight broils. It is, in fact, but another name for a *rowdy* or *loafer*. The name comes from their wearing long side-locks, which they are said to smear with soap. [Bartlett]

socdologer

A decisive blow; one, in the slang language, capable of setting a man thinking. [Dunglison] This strange word is probably a perversion in spelling and pronunciation of *doxology,* a stanza sung at the close of religious services, and as a sign of dismissal. Hence, *socdolager* is a conclusive argument; the winding up of a debate; a settler; and figuratively, in a contest, a heavy blow, which shall bring it to a close. [Bartlett]

soda-prairie

A plain covered with an efflorescence of soda, elsewhere called *natron.* These plains, of great extent, are found in New Mexico, Texas, and Arizona. [Bartlett]

sold his saddle

Since a cowpuncher's saddle is tailored to the individual's particular anatomy, it will be the last item he will part with if hard put to it for cash. Therefore, when one says he has *sold his saddle,* it means he is really broke and can't get a loan. The meaning is sometimes carried still further to indicate disgrace or betrayal of a trust, or even to suggest laziness. [Tallman]

some punkins

Said of those who are pretentious. "He thinks he's *some punkins.*" Western New York, Nebraska. [Bowen] The pumpkin, because of its habit of growing sometimes to prodigious size, has given origin to the facetious phrase *some pumpkins.* [Krapp]

some scissors

Of some account. "He spoke proudly, with *some scissors.*" Aroostook County, Maine. [Carr]

sonnywhacks

A good-natured form of address to the ship's boys, and used to boys alongshore. [Colcord]

sons of wax

Boot and shoemakers. *Sons of wax* is neither an uncommon nor an uncomplimentary name for them, although the address "How are you, my *sons-of-waxes*?" . . . can hardly be excused. [Schele De Vere]

soup bunch

A small bundle of vegetables for soup. Louisiana, Georgia. [Rontt]

sozzle

A sluttish woman; one that spills water and other liquids carelessly. New England. [Webster]

spang

An expletive signifying fullness or completeness of action, like the occasional use of the word *full*. [Thornton] "Every now and then I run *spang* agin' sumbody." [Jones]

sparked it

Courting; young men keeping company with young women and sitting by the fire after the family has gone to bed. [Humphreys] *Sparkin'*, courting. "What girl were you *sparkin'* last Sunday?" Kentucky. [Fruit]

spark in the throat

A desire for liquor. [Weseen]

spasmodics

"[He] was so thunderstruck that he came near having the *spasmodics*." North Carolina. [Eliason]

speaking image

Exact likeness. "He's the *speakin' image* of his daddy." Eastern Alabama. [Payne]

speck and applejees

Pork fat and apples cut up and cooked together. An old-fashioned Dutch dish (*spek en appeltjes*) still made in New York. [Bartlett]

spill the soup

To reveal a secret. [Weseen]

spindigo

Said of one who has come out badly, as from an examination at college or a speculation on the stock exchange. Probably from the English army slang *spin,* to reject from an examination, *spindle,* the third swarm of bees from a hive, [and] *spinny,* thin, slender. To this, some facetious person has probably added *indigo,* to give it a sufficiently blue tone. [Schele de Vere]

split finger

A clerk or white-collar worker, one whose hands are unaccustomed to manual labor and who would suffer from blistered split fingers if forced into hard work. [Irwin]

split the blanket

Of a married pair, to separate. Northwest Arkansas. [Carr] "They *split the blanket* after living together ten years." Southeastern Missouri. [Crumb] Sometimes one hears *split the quilt.* Ozarks. [Randolph & Wilson]

splorum

Much ado about nothing—much cry and little wool. Or in the Yankee dialect, "all talk and no cider." [Farmer]

spondulicks

A term for specie or money. It would appear to have some connection with Dutch *spaunde,* "chips," also slang for money; and there is a word *oolik,* bad, wretched. The term probably originated in New York in some confusion or perversion of these words. This term has become common among English turfites. "I'm derned if I'd live two miles out o' town. . . . Not for his *spondulicks.*" —Mark Twain's *Huckleberry Finn.* [Barrère]

sporting house

A house of bad repute. Northwest Arkansas. [Carr]

Sporting women, an Americanism for gay women. [Johnson]

sposh

A mixture of mud or snow and water. Central Connecticut. [Mead]

spotted lands

The lands of Missouri were called *spotted lands*—one strip was good and another bad. [Thornton]

spring-bag

A New England farmer's term used of the filling udders of cows when about to calve. [Farmer]

spring poor

Said of animals when lean in the spring. Maine, northern New Hampshire. [England]

Spud Islanders

A native or resident of Prince Edward Island . . . so called because it is famous for its potatoes. [Scargill]

squaddle

"Put your feet in your slippers. I don't like to see you *squaddling* about like that." Ontario. [Chamberlain]

squantum

The name of a species of fun known to the Nantucket folks, which is thus described by the New York *Mirror*: "A party of ladies and gentlemen go to one of the famous watering-places of resort, where they fish, dig clams, talk, laugh, sing, dance, play, bathe, sail, eat and have a general good time. . . . Care is thrown to the wind, politics discarded, war ignored, pride humbled, stations levelled, wealth scorned, virtue exalted, and this is *squantum*." Probably from Indian place-names, as one in or near Quincy, Massachusetts. [Bartlett] A common expression in New England is, "She looks as if she came from *Squan-*

tum," from some rustic out-of-the-way place. [Barrère] It has been suggested that this term may have been borrowed from Boston, as Squantum is the name of a peninsula jutting into the harbor about six miles south of the city, formerly a favorite resort for a day's picnic outing. [Macy]

squaw winter

A short period preceding the Indian summer, or else occurring after spring has set in. [Thornton] An early cold snap accompanied by flurries of snow. [Monroe]

squee-jawed

Crooked; irregular. "Thet there smokehouse is plum *squee-jawed.*" Ozarks. [Randolph] *Squelopperjawed,* crooked; askew. [Berrey]

squeeze the biscuit

To catch the saddlehorn when riding. *Shaking hands with grandma,* synonymous with *pulling leather,* [*grabbin' the nubbin* and *reaching for the apple*] . . . to grab the saddlehorn during the riding of an unruly horse. West. [R. Adams] *Squeeze Lizzie,* to grasp the saddlehorn. . . . *Hunt leather,* to hold on to the saddle while riding a bucking horse. [Berrey]

squeeze the biscuit

squidged

Subsided. "His hand was all swoll up, but now it's all *squidged* down." North Carolina. [Kephart]

squirrel-headed

Narrow-minded. Arkansas. [Hanford]

squirt your dye

This means, "Now do your best. Your time for action has come." A phrase borrowed from the dyer's workshop. [Barrère] *Squirt your dye-stuff,* to go on speaking, even when what you have to say is bad. Southwestern Wisconsin. [Savage]

squizzle

To let squizzle, to fire a gun. [Mathews]

squoze

Squeezed. Snake County, Missouri. [Taylor]

staddles

Clumps of trees. Oregon. [Thornton]

stamfish

To talk in a way not generally understood. [Matsell]

stand Sam

An Americanism for to "stand treat," which originated among the soldiers during the Civil War. . . . They demanded liquor by wholesale, saying that Uncle Sam would pay for it, and it was everyone's duty to *stand Sam*. [Johnson]

started and sprung

In the early stage of intoxication. "He's *started and sprung*." Eastern Maine. [Carr]

start your boots

An Americanism for "Be off!" [Johnson]

steam doctor

A doctor who treats all or most diseases with hot water and vapor baths. [Craigie]

steam fiddle, horse piano

A calliope. Circus and carnival slang. [Weseen]

stick floats

If that's the way your stick floats, if that's what you mean. The "stick" is tied to the beaver trap by a string and, floating on the water, points out its position, should a beaver have carried it away. [Ruxton]

stivver

To get moving. A mother would say to her boy, "Now *stivver* along to the store and don't be all day about it." Sometimes it was used to describe hard going. An old lady might sigh and say, "Well, I'll manage to *stivver* along somehow." New England. [Haywood]

stock and block

Entirely. [Thornton]

stone jacket

A prison; "dressed in a *stone jacket.*" [Thornton]

stoop tobacco

Cigar and cigarette ends picked up in the streets, the picker having to stoop over to reach them. [Irwin]

store pay

Pay[ment] in goods from a store instead of in cash. Central Connecticut. [Mead]

stranger's fever

A fever to which newcomers into an area are thought to be particularly subject. [Mathews]

strawberry friend

A moocher. Many city people visit their backwoods cousins only when strawberries are ripe to get enough free berries for a year's supply of jam. Ozarks. [Randolph & Wilson]

striped pig

The legislature of Massachusetts, which state is a stronghold of the [Temperence] Society, passed an act last year by which it prohibited the selling of spirits in a smaller quantity than fifteen gallons, intending thereby to do away with the means of dram-drinking at the groceries, as they are termed. A clause, however, permitted apothecaries to retail smaller quantities, and the consequence was that all the grog-shops commenced taking out apothecaries' licenses. That being stopped, the "striped pig" was resorted to; that is to say, a man charged people the value of a glass of liquor "to see a striped pig," which peculiarity was exhibited as a sight, and when in the house, the visitors were offered a glass of spirits for nothing. [Marryat] A *blue pig* is a place where whiskey is surreptitiously sold. [Tucker]

striped pig

strollopin'
Highly satisfactory. "Jeff shore has made hisse'f some *strollopin'* good liquor." Ozarks. [Randolph]
suability
Liable to be sued. Several years ago, when the question—whether a state could be sued—was under discussion, the word was much used. [Pickering]

sugar in one's spade

Smooth and polite conduct on the part of one who seeks to gain something. [Thornton]

sugar off

The verb to *sugar off* is derived from the custom of eating the maple sugar as it is poured off in its hot state on the snow around, thus making a dainty compound resembling ice cream, which at home is often produced by a similar mixture with tree-molasses. . . . To *sugar off* is one of those expressions the thoroughbred Yankee rolls as a sweet morsel under his tongue when speaking of a large fortune or rich inheritance. Thus we find it in a recent notice of a humorous author: "Josh Billings, who comes of a wealthy family . . . estimated that his estate would *sugar off*, as they say in Vermont, about $200,000." —*Harper's Bazar*, 1871. [Thornton]

suit of hair

Suit, as applied to hair, is probably an Americanism. In the South, a lady is said to possess a wonderfully fine *suit of hair*. [Schele de Vere]

Sunday school show

A circus that has eliminated dishonest concessions and gambling devices. Circus and carnival slang. [Weseen]

Sunday school words

Oaths, curses. "I felt like going off and saying some *Sunday school words*." Northwest Arkansas. [Carr]

sundowner

A tramp . . . who blows in to some Western camp about sunset asking for work, which he knows cannot be obtained at that hour, but who is usually accommodated with rest and refreshment. Sometimes called a whaler from his habit of cruising about the country. Western Canada. [Sandilands]

sun-grins

The seeming smiles of a person whose face is not protected against the sun's rays. Northwest Arkansas. [Carr]

sun-hound

An illusory sun, seen when [reflected] in the ice. Newfoundland. [England]

surface-coal

Cow dung, which is widely used for fuel. West Texas. [Rollins] *Prairie pancakes,* dried manure used as fuel. [Berrey] *Bois de vache,* buffalo chips . . . frequently written *bodewash* by Americans. Mississippi River Valley. [McDermott]

swallow one's teeth

To retract a statement. "I made him *swallow his teeth*." Northwest Arkansas. [Carr]

swaddler

In America, this term is specially applied to men who are paid by pickpockets to preach in public places and collect a crowd in which they may ply their craft. In America, men who pick a quarrel with a man and, at the same time, beat and rob him. . . . In old cant, a *swaddler* was a pedlar. [Barrère]

swiddle

To stir; to dip. "He kept *a-swiddlin'* his finger in the soup." Ozarks. [Randolph]

swilge

To wash, to rinse, as a woman may *swilge* a churn. In some quarters to *swilge out* means to take a vaginal douche. Ozarks. [Randolph & Wilson]

swoggle

To dip or stir. "*Swoggle* yer bread in them sogrums." Ozarks. [Randolph]

Everyone knows an Americanism when he sees it. . . . Americanisms are foreign words, and should be so treated.

—English lexicographer and grammarian
Henry Fowler's *The King's English* (1906)

tablespread

A tablecloth. [Clapin]

tackle a horse

To harness, as to *tackle a horse* into a gig, sleigh, coach, or wagon. [Bartlett]

tail goes over the hide

In the days before fixed prices, a clothing merchant, asked to include a pair of suspenders with a suit of clothes just purchased, hesitated at first and then acquiesced, saying, "Oh well, take 'em. *The tail goes with the hide.*" The expression is from selling slaughtered beef. Southwestern Wisconsin. [Savage]

tail over the dashboard

"Head up and tail over the dashboard," in a lively, spirited way. Western Indiana. [Brown]

take for the kitchen

To withdraw from the conversation; to remain silent. A

neighbor told me, "Them fellers got to talkin' purty deep with big words an' all, so I just *tuck for the kitchen*." He did not actually leave the room but he declined to take part in the conversation. Ozarks. [Randolph & Wilson]

take in wood

In the West, where steam navigation is so abundant, when they ask you to drink they say, "Stranger, will you *take in wood*?"—the vessels taking in wood as fuel to keep the steam up, and the person taking in spirits to keep *his* steam up. [Marryat]

take my hat

In the United States, when any man narrates a story which is so incredible or extravagant that the auditor must confess that he cannot outdo it, the latter often exclaims, "Take my hat!" . . . "Saw my leg off" was an equivalent for the same phrase. [Barrère]

take the rag off the bush

To outdo. From the fact that, not unfrequently at shooting matches in the West, a target is improvised with a rag hung on a bush. [Clapin]

talk to one's plate

To "say grace." Eastern Kentucky. [Shearin]

talking-iron

A comical name for a gun or rifle. [Bartlett] *One-eyed scribe,* a Texas term for a revolver. . . . *Five-shooter* and *six-shooter* are, doubtless, quite familiar to English ears, but not some of the Texan names for the weapon: *meat-in-the-pot, blue lightning, peace-maker, Mr. Speaker, black-eyed Susan, pill box,* and *my unconverted friend.* [Farmer]

talk underground

To talk low and indistinctly. Cape Cod. [Chase]

tantoaster

This is the singular name in some parts of Maine for a gale or storm. [Farmer]

teacherage

A cottage for the teacher, built close to the rural schoolhouse. Western Washington. [Garrett] *Teacherage* is analagous to *parsonage*. Kansas. [Ruppenthal]

teetotataciously

A Western form, supposed to be an emphatic variant of *teetotal*. [Farmer]

ten-cent man

A small, narrow-minded, or trifling man. [Barrère]

ten-strike

A knocking down of ten pins at one throw of a ball; a thorough work. [Bartlett] Applied to a very lucky hit at anything, or to an unusual stroke of success. [Barrère] *Ten-strikers,* men who, in the conflict between North and South, boasted they were an equal match for ten Yankees. The phrase was first introduced by Lieut. J. W. Boothe of the Seventh Texas Battalion, and at once leaped into popular and general use. [Farmer]

terawchy

This word is evidently of Dutch origin, and would seem to be *te ratje,* the little rat, an equivalent term for the "creeping mouse," which is used in a like manner. It is a very common word in the nursery and is always accompanied by a peculiar motion of the fingers, with the palm of the hand presented to the child. It is as well known among the old English families of New York as among those of Dutch descent. [Bartlett]

tetnit

A child born of elderly parents. Weare, New Hampshire. [England]

Texas butter

The cowboy's name for gravy. Put some flour into the grease in which the steak was fried, and let it bubble and brown; then add hot water and stir until it thickens. [R. Adams] *Skid grease,* butter. Loggers' and miners' slang. [Weseen] *Bear's butter,* fat of the bear used in cooking, medicines, cosmetics, and for insulating the body against the cold. Canada. [Scargill]

Texian

A Texan. "An official variant of the word *Texan,* which enjoyed wide popular usage during the ten years of the Republic of Texas. . . . After the Civil War, a new generation allowed the old spelling to fall into disuse—much to the disgust of many old *Texians.*" —Randolph Adams's *Dictionary of American History,* 1940. Also *Texasian, Texican.* [Craigie]

thatchy

Said of milk, the milk tastes *thatchy* because the cows eat thatch. A long, coarse grass growing in the salt marshes is known as *thatch* on the New Hampshire and Massachusetts seacoast. If it was ever used for roofing it is no longer so used. Portsmouth, New Hampshire. [Allen]

them'uns

Probably due to the analogy of *we'uns* and *you'uns,* which are more common. North Carolina. [Steadman]

this child

Myself. An expression much used by negroes, and occasionally by white people. "You've got *this child* into a tarnation scrape." —*Knickerbocker* magazine, 1843. [Thornton] *Himself,* used for the head of a family. "The whole Bailey Loring tribe—*himself,* madame, and Sally." [Atkinson]

thousand-mile shirt

The shirt of a railroad boomer [laborer] was often given this title because, as an itinerant worker, he traveled light and supposedly wore the same shirt for thousands of miles. [Tallman]

thousand of brick

"Like a *thousand of brick*," an Americanism for *very heavily*, as if a waggon-load of bricks had been dumped down on one. [Johnson] "He came down on my foot like a *thousand of brick*." Cape Cod. [Chase] *Thousands*, a large size or amount rather than a large number. "Them britches is *thousands* big, but they ain't noways long 'nuff." Ozarks. [Randolph]

three twenty-nine

During the presidential campaign of 1880, these numbers were chalked by Democrats on every wall, doorstep, and fence in the land. Mr. Garfield, the Republican candidate, had been charged with having received a bribe of $329 worth of Credit Mobilier stock. [Norton]

through the cabin window

A shipmaster who began his sea career as an officer is said to have "come in through the cabin window." [Colcord]

thunder flurry

Thunder. North Carolina. [Eliason]

thunderingly

Very. "He is *thunderingly* scientific." [Atkinson]

tick-nation

A name given to regions in which ticks abound; and, as the grasses and sandy soil infected by them are peculiar to the poorer parts of the country, it is sometimes used as a term of reproach. [Bartlett]

tidewalker

A water-soaked log with only one end out of water; hence, a drifter, a ne'er-do-well. The steamship man's name for it is "propeller-inspector." [Colcord]

tie one to that

After finishing a tale, a Western storyteller may conclude his turn with this expression, throwing a challenge to the next narrator to outdo him. [Tallman]

tie-ticket

"To take a *tie-ticket*" means to walk the railroad ties. Northwest Arkansas. [Carr]

tight scrouging

For *difficult*. Georgia. [Sherwood]

tillicums

Folks. Pacific Northwest. [Garrett]

timber-beast

A lumberman. Coast of Washington and Oregon. [Lehman]

time of books

The study period in school. A teacher told me that she whipped a boy "for hollerin' in *time o' books*." Ozarks. [Randolph & Wilson]

tinclad

A musket-proof gunboat such as were used on the American rivers during the Civil war, the armor-plating of these being very light. Nowadays, however, the word *tin-clad* is in common use in the Western building trade as an adjective in reference to frame houses, vehicles, doors, or household fittings that have been encased in a covering of tin. [Sandilands]

tippybobs

A contemptuous term for the wealthy classes. [Bartlett]

tip-toe Nancy

An affected girl putting on airs. Maine, northern New Hampshire. [England]

toadskins

Paper money; an old term, and of relatively rare use, *scratch, jack,* or *kale* usually replacing it. [Irwin] Apparently from "greenback." [Kane]

toesmithing

Dancing. Theater slang. [Weseen]

tom-dog

Male dogs as well as cats take the prefix "tom" in some parts of the West. [Bartlett]

tom-dog

too previous

A *little too previous,* an Americanism for being in too great a hurry; rushing at conclusions; saying or doing a thing without sufficient warranty. [Johnson]

tooth carpenter

A dentist. Arkansas. [Hanford]

tooth-jumper

A mountain dentist of the old school who extracts teeth

by means of a mallet and a slender steel punch. Ozarks. [Randolph] *Tooth-jumping*, extracting a tooth by causing it to *jump* out with one blow of a hammer or mallet on a nail or punch held at an angle against the tooth. North Carolina. [Wentworth]

tophet, tunkit
Defined originally as the place of abominations, the very gate or pit of hell. Hence, boys used to say, "I'll see you in *Tophet* before I'll do it." [Bartlett] *Tunkit*, a meaningless term used for *devil, hell,* etc. "Who in *tunket.* . . ." [Thornton] "My head aches like *tunkit*," like everything. Central New York. [Monroe]

to-rights
To-rights, with the adverbial *s,* which in England means excellent, used to be employed in the United States instead of *directly.* This use of the word has, however, become obsolete here as well as in England, and the phrase is now used only in the sense of "putting things *to-rights*," setting things in order. [Schele de Vere]

Tory peas
English peas. North Carolina. [Eliason]

to the halves
It means either to let or to hire a piece of land, the lessee and lessor receiving half the profit in money and half in kind. This New England colloquialism . . . still survives in America, though it is obsolete in England. [Farmer]

towno!
A very ancient term in Nantucket, being the call for help from town raised by the lookout from the shore whaling stations when whales were sighted. Nantucket. [Macy]

traditionate
To indoctrinate; to teach by tradition. [Thornton]

trampoosing

Traversing. [Humphrey] *Trampoose,* an enlargement of the English "to tramp," is a genuine Americanism, and means to wander about listlessly. "The sergeant has successfully *trampoosed* this, the whole South." [Schele de Vere] Perhaps from the French *trépigner,* to stamp with the feet. [Bartlett]

trottleoxing

Gadding about; similar to *traipsing.* Nantucket. [Macy]

trouters' special

A train of several cars which left St. John's on the eve of the 24th of May with trouters for the various ponds of their choice, dropping them off wherever they wished along the railway line and picking them up the following night to bring them back with their catches, hangovers, fly-bites, chills, etc. Newfoundland. [Story]

trowsaloons

A humorous combination of *trousers* and *pantaloons.* Virginia. [Thornton]

tuckout

One's fill. "I pounded up them clam shells for the hens, and they had a great *tuckout.*" Cape Cod. [Chase]

tug-mutton

A child; from the days of sheep-stealing. "He's got a wife and a dozen *tug-muttons.*" Southwestern Wisconsin. [Savage]

turkey on one's back

A drunken man is sometimes said to have a "turkey on his back." Perhaps the allusion to his having won one at a raffle in a drinking-place. [Bartlett]

turn of the night

Passing midnight. "We heard you slip in towards the *turn*

of the night." Virginia. [Dingus] The depressing hour of the night when those who are sick are supposed to be most likely to die. Some time after midnight. Southeastern Missouri. [Crumb]

turnscrew

A screwdriver. Newfoundland. [England]

twist and tucking

"The whole *twist and tucking,*" the whole kit and caboodle. [Craigie]

twistical

Not quite moral. [Humphreys] *Twistical* denotes in slang that which has a moral twist, and is hence unfair and not straightforward. New England. [Schele de Vere]

two by four

Small, in disparagement; perhaps in allusion to the dimensions *two by four,* the smallest lumber used for framework. "A lot of *two by four* politicians are yelling their heads off." Kansas, Pennsylvania, Southeast. [Ruppenthal]

two lamps burning and no ship at sea

An old saying used as a rebuke for extravagance of any kind. Nantucket. [Macy]

two-ten

A veiled warning called by a clerk to his followers to say that a kleptomaniac had come into the shop. "Keep your *two* eyes on his *ten* fingers," is the import of the expression. Newfoundland. [Devine]

The privilege of barbarizing the King's English is assumed by all ranks and conditions of men. . . . Unless the present progress of change be arrested by an increase of taste and judgment in the more educated classes, there can be no doubt that in another century the dialect of the Americans will become utterly unintelligible to an Englishman, and that the nation will be cut off from the advantages arising from their participation in British literature.

—English army captain Thomas Hamilton's
Men and Manners in America (1833)

under hatches

When in trouble or distress, thieves report themselves as being *under hatches*. The simile is drawn from seafaring life. [Farmer]

underpinners

The legs, which in English flash language are called *pins*. [Bartlett]

under the window

Nantucketeers never sit *at* the window or *by* the window, but always *under* the window. There is perhaps no phrase which is more often noted in our speech than this, and we who use it are often asked to explain, or even to demonstrate, just how we sit under the window. The answer is that as Nantucket windows are usually rather high from the floor, as we sit by or at one of them, we are *under* them, just as the wallpaper or the baseboard . . . is under them. [Macy]

unhandsome fix

Uncomfortable. [Trollope]

unhidebound

Lax of maw; capacious. [Webster] Not having the skin fitting closely, as is the case when animals are swoln and full. [Hunter]

United Statesian

A citizen of, or dweller in, the United States. [Craigie] *Unitedstatish*, English, as used in the United States. *Talk United States*, to speak the American form of English. [Weseen]

up Green River

A very odd expression, confined mainly to the mountaineers in the wilder parts of the Southwest, is quite expressive. They say they "send a man *up Green River*" when they have killed him. The phrase had its origin in a once famous factory on Green River, where a superior kind of large knife was made, very popular among hunters and trappers. On the blade the words "Green River Works" were engraved, and hence the mountaineers, using the knife to dispatch an adversary, literally sent his blood *up Green River*. [Schele de Vere]

up jib

To start off. "As soon as I told him that, he *up jib* and went off." Cape Cod. [Chase]

uppers 'n unders

False teeth. Maine, northern New Hampshire. [England]

upscuddle

Quarrel. North Carolina. [Kephart]

upsee-Dutch

An old phrase signifying "in the Dutch manner or style," as "to drink *upsee-Dutch*," to drink in the Dutch manner, that is to drink deeply. From Dutch *op-zyn-Deutsch,* in the Dutch fashion. [Lyons]

ups with

Used colloquially for *raises.* "She *ups with* the broom and gives it to him in the head." Newfoundland. [Devine]

up the spout

Perhaps the only commercial term that ever became a universal favorite in the army is *going up the spout,* which was used in the Confederate army almost exclusively for any disasterous conclusion of an enterprise, as well as for the loss of an article. A man's mule that had strayed away from camp was said to have *gone up the spout,* and the Confederacy itself, after the surrender of Richmond, had simply *gone up.* The figure of speech is taken from the spout, or tin tube, up which pawnbrokers send ticketed articles to be kept till redeemed in the upper part of the house. [Schele de Vere]

up to the handle

In dead earnest. "He's courting her right *up to the handle.*" Eastern Maine. [Carr]

up to the handle

In the mining districts of California and Nevada, many strange words and phrases have sprung into existence, some of which have so taken root that they are heard in the colloquial language of the towns and cities, and have even crept into the ephemeral literature of the Pacific States. By no writers has this peculiar idiom been so much employed as by Bret Harte and Mark Twain. In speaking of the language of the mining regions, the latter says, "The slang of Nevada is the richest and most infinitely varied and copious that ever existed anywhere in the world, perhaps, except for the mines of California in the 'early days.' It was hard to preach a sermon without it and be understood."

—John Bartlett, in the preface to the fourth edition of his
Dictionary of Americanisms (1877), quoting
from Mark Twain's *Roughing It*

Vs and Xs

Five and ten dollar bills. The former were occasionally called *V spots*. "My wallet [was] distended with *Vs* and *Xs* to its utmost capacity." —*Knickerbocker* magazine, January, 1837. [Thornton] Much used in making bets, as "I'll bet you a *V*." [Bartlett] *V*, a five-year [prison] sentence. . . . *Nickle note,* a five dollar bill. Merely a play on the word *nickel* for a five-cent piece. [Irwin]

vamp it

To walk. Newfoundland. [England]

verse about

A verse or two by each reader in turn. "Reading the Scriptures *verse about,* . . . a custom in many Christian families; . . . that is, each member of the families reading a verse or two in turn until the whole chapter is finished." —*New York Observer.* [Bartlett]

Virginia fence

"To make a *Virginia fence*" means to walk like a drunken man, in humorous allusion to the zigzag shape of a "snake-fence." [Schele de Vere] "He's laying a *snake-fence,*" used to describe the gait of a drunken man. Western Pennsylvania. [Hart]

volleydo

A swing or merry-go-round. New Orleans. [Routh]

voter-cooping

To coop voters is to collect them, as it were, in a coop or cage so as to be sure of their services on election day. Liquor dealers are the usual "coopers," for obvious reasons. [Farmer] Collecting and confining them several days previous to an election in a house or on a vessel hired for the purpose. Here they are treated with good living and liquors, and at a proper day are taken to the polls and "voted," as it is called, for the party. [Bartlett]

vum

"I *vum*!" for "I vow!" is a euphemistic form of oath often heard in New England. . . . "I *snum!*" a New England euphemism for "I swear." [Bartlett] *Swow,* "I *swow,*" I swear. [Trollope]

Even our [English] newspapers, hitherto regarded as models of correct literacy style, . . . are lending countenance to what at first sight appears a monstrously crude and almost imbecile jargon; while others, fearful of a direct plunge, modestly introduce the uncouth bantlings with a saving clause. The phrase, "as the Americans say," might in some cases be ordered from the typefoundry as a logotype, so frequently does it do introduction duty.

—Englishman John S. Farmer, in the preface to his
Americanisms Old and New (1889)

wabash

To cheat. This term, though undoubtedly of Indian origin, is uncertain in derivation. [Farmer] "He's *wabashed*," meaning he is cheated, is an expression much used in Indiana and other parts of the West. [Bartlett]

wadgetty

Fidgety; nervous. Nantucket. [Macy]

wake the wrong passenger

To make a mistake in [recognizing an] individual. A modern substitute for the old phrase "to get the wrong sow by the ear." The allusion is to the custom on board steamboats [and later trains] of arousing or waking passengers at stopping-places at night, when frequent mistakes are made and the wrong person called up. [Bartlett] "To get the wrong pig by the tail," the Yankee equivalent of . . . "to wake the wrong passenger," and "to bark up the wrong tree." [Farmer]

walk uphill

To be pregnant is to *walk uphill* in southern Illinois. [Mencken]

walk the chalk

An Americanism for to act straight or keep in the right path. [Johnson]

walk turkey

To strut, and idiomatically, to be unsteady in gait. [Farmer]

wany-edged

[Of a board] not of even thickness, but varying because of the round outside surface of the log. Kansas. [Ruppenthal]

wapper-jawed

Crooked. "The curtain is *wapper-jawed*." Western Ohio. [Hart]

watch one's corners

To keep a sharp look out; to be shrewdly attentive. The expression comes in this way: when a man is ploughing, and reaches the corners of his land, he must be careful in

watch one's corners

turning his team and plough or he will not break up the land thoroughly at the corners. [Clapin]

water-haul

A cheat; a swindle. A conjectural explanation may be offered. The hauling of goods by water being cheaper than by land, contractors would employ water carriage and charge the government [for] land-carriage. [Thornton]

water-wagon

"To be on the *water-wagon*," to abstain from hard drinks. New York. [Monroe]

way-train

A train which stops at intermediate stations. "He descended, sleepy and sore, from a *way-train*." —Mark Twain's *The Gilded Age*. [Ramsay]

wear the bustle wrong

To be pregnant. Kansas. [Ruppenthal]

weasel words

A statement that changes the fundamental meaning of a previous statement. [Weseen] Words that suck the life out of the words next to them, just as a weasel sucks an egg and leaves the shell. —Stewart Chaplin, *Century* magazine, 1900.

wedding trees

A term throughout New England for the pair of stately elms a newly-married couple planted by their front door. Mainers liked to call them "marriage elms." [Gould]

wee-waw

Shaky, loose, rickety. "The old wagon was *weewawing* all over the road." Maine, northern New Hampshire. [England] Aslant and askew, not plumb or vertical. Also *eeyaw*. Used for quirks and oddities in the same sense as warp. Maine. [Gould]

wet quaker

One who is a dram-drinker on the sly. [Thornton]

whales on

Much devoted to, as "John is *whales on* the new girl." [Weseen]

whapperknocker

The *whapperknocker* is somewhat bigger than a weazel, and of a beautiful brown-red color. Connecticut. [Peters]

What's the matter with Hannah!

A street catch-phrase with no especial meaning. For a time, it rounded off every statement of fact or expression of opinion among the vulgar. [Farmer]

where the woodbine twineth

To go *where the woodbine* [honeysuckle] *twineth* is to sink into obscurity. [Thornton]

whick-whack

To dash hither and yon. "He was *whick-whacking* back and forth, from house to barn all day." [From English dialect *whick*, quick.] Nantucket. [Macy]

while my head is hot

As long as I live. Southeastern Missouri. [Crumb]

whip-sawing

The acceptance of fees or bribes from two opposing persons or parties. It is believed to have originated in the New York Assembly, and is evidently derived from the whip-saw of mechanics, which "cuts both ways." [Norton]

whisky-boy

A person responsible for dispensing the liquor at a barn-raising, logging-bee, etc. [Scargill]

white hen's chicken

Extremely pleasant or desirable persons. "Sue thought Hy was one o' the *white hen's chickens*." Maine, northern New Hampshire. [England]

white in one's eye

An irritable disposition. "He's got lots of *white in his eye*." Northwest Arkansas. [Carr]

white-light district

An amusement district; a theatrical district; Broadway, New York City. [Berrey]

whitleather stage

At the age of an old maid; [from] *whitleather,* cured but untanned hide. North Carolina. [Cooper]

whittlety-whet

When two are running a race, we say, "It's a *whittlety-whet* who will get there first." Kentucky. [Fruit]

whole cloth

A tale which is a lie from beginning to end is said to be made up out of the *whole cloth.* [Thornton]

whole-footed

Whole-footed [is] used with a profusion and want of discrimination which has utterly destroyed [its] original meaning. Any devising man who invites a crowd to "drinks all around" is instantly praised as a "*whole-footed* man." [Schele de Vere]

wickiup

Any meagre shelter improvised of brush, boughs, etc. Used by woodsmen. Pacific Northwest. [Lehman]

wilcox

To pass a restless, uneasy, sleepless night. "I *wilcoxed* all night long." Nantucket. [Macy]

wild fowl flavor

Tasty and appetizing food was said to have a real *wild fowl flavor.* The dish in question might be a pie or any kind of food. Nantucket. [Macy]

wild train

A railroad train not on the timetables. [Bartlett]

wind has January

"The *wind has January* in it," cold weather. Pacific Northwest. [McCulloch]

wind is out

In Connecticut, a curious usage of *out* is colloquial. "The wind is out," [meaning it] comes from outward—the sea. [Farmer]

winoes

Workers employed in the grape harvest, or those employed in a vineyard. The term is frequently employed in the West, seldom in the East. [Irwin]

wire-road

A highway along which a telegraph extends. Northwest Arkansas. [Carr]

with-its

The other things served at dinner—the vegetables, pickles, dessert, etc. Hence, there will be a roast of beef and *with-its*. Maine. [Gould]

with squirrel

Pregnancy is seldom mentioned when both men and women are present. . . . If no women are about, a hillman may remark to a comparative stranger that his wife is *ketched,* or *pizened,* or *springin',* or *sprung,* or *too big for her clothes,* or *knocked up,* or *comin' fresh* . . . or *with squirrel.* . . . At Granby, Missouri, when a man's wife was about to be delivered of a child, a friend said to the husband, "Well, Tom, it looks like your bees are a-swarmin'." To say that a woman is *about to find pups* means she is going to have a baby. Ozarks. [Randolph & Wilson]

witness-trees

In newly settled countries [of] the West, every square mile is marked by . . . trees, and the corners especially distinguished by stakes, whose place is pointed out by trees called *witness trees*. [Bartlett]

womblecropped

Uncomfortable. "I feel a great deal *womblecropped* about dropping her acquaintance." —*Massachusetts Spy*, September 5, 1798. [Thornton]

wooden swearing

Showing anger by acts of violence or roughness, as knocking furniture about. Kansas. [Ruppenthal]

woods-colt

A horse of uncertain paternity. Also applied to a person of illegitimate birth. Missouri. [Crumb] *Catch colt*, a foal of unknown paternity. Western Canada. [Sandilands]

wood-up

The enormous steamboats of the Ohio and the Mississippi require such vast supplies of fuel for their long journeys that in early spring, detachments of men are set ashore at convenient places, whose duty it is to cut wood, pile it up on the shore, and carry it on board the boat that has engaged their services. . . . The boats necessarily stop often to *wood-up*, as the term is, and tie up to a wooding-place. The passengers avail themselves of the opportunity to take a stroll on shore to examine the snakes and vipers—which are apt to accumulate beneath the huge woodpile—and to take a drink; hence, unfortunately, *to wood* has in the West become a popular euphemistic term for "to take a dram." [Schele de Vere]

woofits

The unpleasant aftereffects of overindulgence, especially drinking. [Berrey]

word with the bark on it

A very expressive word. Western Indiana. [Brown] An ultimatum. Northwest Arkansas. [Carr]

world's people

A phrase originated by the Quakers to signify persons not belonging to their society, and afterwards adopted by some other sects. [Thornton] "If a quaker love a lady out of society, he must ask liberty and pardon for the sin of loving one of the *world's people*." —Arthur Singleton's *Letters from the South and West,* 1824.

writing-gait

"My *writing-gait* is twenty-four words per minute." —Mark Twain's *Simplified Alphabet,* 1899. [Ramsay]

writing-gait

wuzzle

To jumble, muddle, mix. "He *wuzzled* things up in the most singular way." —Harriet Beecher Stowe's *Oldtown Folks,* 1869. [Farmer & Henley]

[The English language] is universally understood and better spoken by the whole mass of people from Georgia to Quebec—an extent of country more than 1200 miles—than by the bulk of people in the different counties of England.

—English "military adventurer" John Harriot's
Struggles Through Life, published in London about 1808

X, cross as

Very cross, or ill-humored. Eastern Alabama. [Payne]

X-eyed

Cross-eyed. *X-legged,* knock-kneed. [Weseen]

XX

A survival, in a somewhat disguised form, of the Latin word *duplex,* which formerly was applied to beer of more than ordinary strength. Thus, the fellows and postmasters of Merton College were forbidden by the statutes to drink *cerevisium duplex,* or strong ale. [Hunter]

I speak for the millions of Englishmen when I say that we are as sick and tired of this so-called "English accent" as you Americans are. It has far less right to be called "standard English" than Yorkshire or any country dialect has—or than any American dialect. . . . I wrote in 1929, "If half the members of each talkie audience shudder every time a silver ghost on the screen says 'Get a load of this,' or 'It's in the bag,' the other half make a note of this wisecrack for future use." I can offer no hope to the professors who think that talkies in pure English prose and verse would stem the Yankee tide. For every such professor there are a thousand talkie fans to whom American has become as intelligible as Cockney, and much more pleasing. There has never been a talkie in pure English prose and there never will be.

—Englishman W. H. Seaman, from the article
"The Awful English of England," published in the
American Mercury (September 1933)

yard-wand
This term is still sometimes used by old people for what we call a *yard-stick*. Anciently it was called a *mete-yard*. [Pickering]

yellow-quarter
A five-dollar gold piece. [Thornton]

yoette

A young girl who served in the naval reserve force during the [First] World War was called a *yoette,* a *yeomanette,* or a *yeowoman.* Sailors' slang. [Weseen]

yooper

An emphatic affirmative, said to be of Cherokee origin. "Is that gal purty? *Yooper!*" Ozarks. [Randolph & Wilson]

York Island

The City of New York . . . is built at the extreme point of Manhattan, or York Island, which is thirteen miles long and from one to two miles wide. . . . The population is 120,000. [Fearon]

The Americans are going to be the most fluent and melodious-voiced people in the world, and the most perfect users of words. . . . I see that the time is nigh when the etiquette of saloons is to be discharged from that great thing, the renovated English speech in America. The occasions of the English speech in America are immense, profound—stretch over ten thousand vast cities, over millions of miles of meadows, farms, mountains, men, through thousands of years. . . . Ten thousand native idiomatic words are growing, or are today already grown, out of which vast numbers could be used by American writers with meaning and effect—words that would be welcomed by the nation, being of the national blood.

—American poet Walt Whitman's lecture "An American Primer,"
written in the early to mid-1850s, and first published
posthumously in *The Atlantic Monthly* (April 1904)

zeppelin in a cloud

Sausage and mashed potatoes. [Fraser] *Dogs in the hay,* frankfurters and sauerkraut. [Berrey]

Dunglison, Robley. "Glossary [of Americanisms]." *Dialect Notes*, 1829–1830.

Edson, H. A., and Edith M. Fairchild. "Word-lists: Tennessee Mountains." *Dialect Notes*, 1895.

Eliason, Norman E. *Tarheel Talk: An Historical Study of the English Language in North Carolina to 1860*. Chapel Hill, NC, 1956.

Ellis, George Edward. *Manuscript of Rhode Island Terms*, c. 1848.

England, George A. "Newfoundland Dialect Items." *Dialect Notes*, 1925.

———. "Rural Locutions of Maine and Northern New Hampshire." *Dialect Notes*, 1914.

Farmer, John S. *Americanisms Old and New: A Dictionary of Words, Phrases, and Colloquialisms Peculiar to the United States, British America, the West Indies, &c.* London, 1889.

——— and W. E. Henley. *Slang and Its Analogues, Past and Present*. London, 1890–1904.

Fearon, Henry Bradshaw. *Sketches of America: A Narrative of a Journey through the Eastern and Western States*. London, 1818.

Fessenden, Thomas Green. "New England Provincialisms," published in *The Ladies' Monitor*. Bellows Falls, VT, 1818.

Ford, P. L. *The Honorable Peter Stirling*. New York, 1894.

Fox, William F. *A History of the Lumber Industry in the State of New York*. Washington, D.C., 1902.

Flint, Timothy. *George Mason the Young Backwoodsman: A Story of the Mississippi*. Boston, 1829.

Fraser, Edward, and John Gibbons. *Soldier and Sailor Words and Phrases, Including . . . British and American War-Words*. London, 1925.

Bibliography

Adams, Charles C. *Boontling: An American Lingo*. Austin, TX, 1971.

Adams, Ramon. *Western Words: A Dictionary of the Range, Cow Camp, and Trail*. Norman, OK, 1944.

Allen, Frederic D. "Contributions to the New England Vocabulary." *Dialect Notes*, c. 1916.

American Dialect Society. *Dialect Notes*. Boston, Norwood, MA; New Haven, CT, 1896–1939.

Atkinson, Caroline P. *The Letters of Susan Hale, 1833–1910*. Boston, 1919.

Atwood, E. Bagby. *The Regional Vocabulary of Texas*. Austin, TX, 1972.

Babbitt, E. H. "The Dialect of Western Connecticut." *Dialect Notes*, 1893.

Barrère, Albert, and Charles Leland. *Dictionary of Slang, Argot, and Cant*. London, 1897.

Bartlett, James. *Dictionary of Americanisms: A Glossary of Words and Phrases Usually Regarded as Peculiar to the United States*. New York, 1848, and Boston, 1877.*

*This text includes only three entries from Bartlett's first edition of 1848, *fire-new*, *sick as a horse*, and *simon-pure*; the rest are from his 1877 edition.

Belknap, Jeremy. *The History of New Hampshire.* Boston, 1793.

Berrey, Lester V., and Melvin Van den Bark. *The American Thesaurus of Slang.* New York, 1942.

Bone, J. H. A. *Petroleum and Petroleum Wells.* Philadelphia, 1865.

Boucher, Jonathan. *Glossary of Archaic and Provincial Words: A Supplement to the Dictionaries of the English Language, Particularly Those of Dr. Johnson and Dr. Webster.* London, c. 1800, 1832.

Bowen, B. L. "A Word-list from Western New York." *Dialect Notes,* 1910.

Breck, Samuel. *Recollections of Samuel Breck, with Passages from his Notebooks.* Philadelphia, 1877.

Briggs, L. B. R. "A Few New England Notes." *Dialect Notes,* c. 1890.

Brockett, John. *A Glossary of North Country Words.* Newcastle-upon-Tyne, 1825.

Brown, Rollo. "A Word-list from Western Indiana." *Dialect Notes,* 1912.

Bruner, Helen, and Frances Francis. "A Short Word-list from Wyoming." *Dialect Notes,* 1912.

Buck, Charles. *A Theological Dictionary.* Philadelphia, 1835.

Carr, Joseph W. "A Word-list from Hampstead, New Hampshire." *Dialect Notes,* 1907.

—— and George D. Chase. "A Word-list from Eastern Maine." *Dialect Notes,* 1907.

Cassidy, Frederic G., and Joan Hall. *Dictionary of Regional American English.* Cambridge, MA, 1985–.

Chamberlain, A. F. "Dialect Research in Canada." *Dialect Notes,* c. 1890.

Chase, George D. "A Word-list from Eastern Maine." *Dialect Notes,* 1913–1914.

——. "Cape Cod Dialect, and Addenda." *Dialect Notes,* 1903–1909.

Chipman, Richard Manning. *Manuscript Notes on Bartlett's Dictionary of Americanisms,* c. 1870.

Clapin, Sylva. *A New Dictionary of Americanisms.* New York, 1902.

Colange, L. *Popular Encyclopedia.* Philadelphia, 1871.

Colcord, Joanna C. *Sea Language Comes Ashore.* New York, 1945.

Combs, Josiah. "Early English Slang Survivals in the Mountains of Kentucky." *Dialect Notes,* 1916–1923.

Cooper, Horton. *North Carolina Mountain Folklore.* Murfreesboro, NC, 1972.

Cornell University Dialect Society. "Words and Phrases." *Dialect Notes,* c. 1900.

Craigie, William, and James Hulbert. *A Dictionary of American English,* Chicago, 1940.

Crumb, D. S. "The Dialect of Southeastern Missouri." *Dialect Notes,* 1903.

Curtiss, Laura C. "Expressions Heard from Chicago People of New England Antecedents." *Dialect Notes,* c. 1910.

Davidson, Robert. *The Presbyterian Church in Kentucky.* New York, 1847.

Devine, Patrick K. *Folk Lore of Newfoundland in Old Words, Phrases, and Expressions.* St. John's, Newfoundland, 1937.

Dingus, L. R. "Appalachian Mountain Words." *Dialect Notes,* 1927.

——. "A Word-list from Virginia." *Dialect Notes,* 1915.

Dixon, W. H. *New America.* London, 1866.

Fruit, John P. "Kentucky Words and Phrases." *Dialect Notes,* 1890–1892.

Garrett, Robert. "A Word-list from the Northwest." *Dialect Notes,* 1919–1920.

Goldin, Hyman E. *Dictionary of American Underworld Lingo.* New York, 1950.

Gould, John. *Maine Lingo: Boiled Owls, Billdads, & Wazzats.* Camden, ME, 1975.

Green, Bennett Wood. *Word-Book of Virginia Folk Speech.* Richmond, VA, 1899.

Greenough, James, and George Kittredge. *Words and Their Ways in English Speech.* New York, 1914.

Grose, Francis. *Classical Dictionary of the Vulgar Tongue.* London, 1796.

Haldeman, Samuel Stehman. *Pennsylvania Dutch: A Dialect of Southern German with an Infusion of English.* London, 1872.

Hale, Edward E. *Gone to Texas: The Wonderful Adventures of a Pullman.* Boston, 1877.

Hall, Benjamin. *A Collection of College Words and Customs.* Cambridge, MA, 1856.

Hamersly, L. R., & Co. *A Naval Encyclopaedia: Comprising a Dictionary of Nautical Words and Phrases; Biographical Notices, and Records of Naval Office.* Philadelphia, 1884.

Hamilton, Thomas. *Men and Manners in America.* London, 1833.

Hanford, G. L. "Metaphor and Simile in American Folk-Speech." *Dialect Notes,* 1918–1927.

Hanley, O. W. "Dialect Words from Southern Indiana." *Dialect Notes,* 1906.

Hart, J. M., et al. "Notes from Cincinnati." *Dialect Notes,* c. 1891.

Harvey, Bartle. "A Word-list from the Northwest." *Dialect Notes,* 1913–1914.

Hayden, Mary Gladys. "A Word-list from Montana." *Dialect Notes,* 1915.

Haywood, Charles F. *Yankee Dictionary: A Compendium of Useful and Entertaining Expressions Indigenous to New England.* Lynn, MA, 1963.

Holland, J. G. *Sevenoaks, a Story of To-day.* New York, 1875.

Hotten, John Camden. *The Slang Dictionary.* London, 1887.

Humphreys, David. Glossary to *The Yankey in England.* Boston, 1815.

Hunter, Robert. *The Encyclopædic Dictionary.* Philadelphia, 1894.

Irving, Washington. *A Knickerbocker's History of New York.* New York, 1809.

Irwin, Godfrey. *American Tramp and Underworld Slang.* London, 1931.

Johnson, Trench H. *Phrases and Names: Their Origins and Meanings.* London, 1906.

Jones, Major. *Sketches of Travel.* Philadelphia, 1848.

Journal of American Folk-Lore. Boston, September 1892.

Kane, Elisha K. "The Jargon of the Underworld." *Dialect Notes,* c. 1927.

Kephart, Horace. "A Word-list from the Mountains of Western North Carolina." *Dialect Notes,* 1917.

Klaeber, Frederick. "A Word-list from Minnesota." *Dialect Notes,* 1913.

Knight, E. H. *Knight's New Mechanical Dictionary.* Boston, 1883.

Krapp, George Philip. *The English Language in America.* New York, 1925.

Lee, Francis B., et al. "Jerseyisms." *Dialect Notes,* 1893.

Lehman, Benjamin. "A Word-list from California." *Dialect Notes,* 1921.

———. "A Word-list from the Northwestern United States." *Dialect Notes,* 1918–1922.

Lowell, James Russell. *The Bigelow Papers.* Boston, 1882.

Lyons, Daniel. *The American Dictionary of the English Language.* New York, 1897.

Macy, William F., and Roland B. Hussey. *The Nantucket Scrap Basket.* Boston, 1930.

Man, A. P. Jr. "Virginia [Word-list]." *Dialect Notes,* 1914.

Marryat, Frederick. *A Diary in America, with Remarks on Its Institutions.* London, 1839.

Massachusetts Historical Society Proceedings. Boston, 1792.

Mathews, Mitford M. *A Dictionary of Americanisms.* Chicago, 1956.

Matsell, George M. *Vocabulum, or The Rogue's Lexicon.* New York, 1859.

Maxfield, Ezra. "Maine List." *Dialect Notes,* 1926.

McCulloch, Walter F. *Woods Words: A Comprehensive Dictionary of Loggers' Terms.* Portland, OR, 1958.

McDermott, John Francis. *A Glossary of Mississippi Valley French, 1673–1850.* St. Louis, 1941.

Mead, William E., and George D. Chase. "A Central Connecticut Word-list." *Dialect Notes,* 1905.

Medbery, James K. *Men and Mysteries of Wall Street.* New York, 1870.

Mencken, Henry Lewis. *The American Language.* New York, 1919.

Mitchell, James. "Nantucketisms of 1848." *American Speech.* New York, Baltimore, 1848.

Monroe, B. S., and Clark Northup. "Some Lumber and Other Words." *Dialect Notes,* c. 1903.

Moorsom, William S. *Letters from Nova Scotia, Comprising Sketches of a Young Country.* London, 1830.

Murray, James, et al. *A New English Dictionary on Historical Principles.* Oxford, 1888–1933.

Northup, Clark S. "Language of the Oil Wells." *Dialect Notes,* 1904.

Norton, Charles Ledyard. *Political Americanisms.* New York, 1890.

Optic, Oliver. *Little Bobtail: Our Boys' and Girls' Monthly.* Boston, 1872.

Palmer, Francis. "Dialect Words from James Fenimore Cooper's *The Pioneers* (1823)." *Dialect Notes,* 1922.

Parry, W. H. "Dialect Peculiarities in Southeastern Ohio." *Dialect Notes,* 1916.

Payne, L. W. Jr. "Word-list from Eastern Alabama and Western Georgia." *Dialect Notes,* 1908–1909.

Pearce, J. W. "Notes from Louisiana." *Dialect Notes,* 1890.

Perrin, P. G. "New England Provincialisms." *Dialect Notes,* 1818.

Peters, Samuel. *A General History of Connecticut.* London, 1781.

Pickering, John. *A Vocabulary . . . Peculiar to the United States.* Boston, 1816.

Pollard, Mary O. "Terms from the Tennessee Mountains." *Dialect Notes,* 1915.

Pound, Louise. "A Second Word-list from Nebraska," with supplement. *Dialect Notes,* 1911, 1916.

Ramsay, Robert L., and Frances G. Emberson. *A Mark Twain Lexicon.* Columbia, MO, 1938.

Randolph, Vance. "A Word-list from the Ozarks." *Dialect Notes,* 1926.

———— and George Wilson. *Down in the Holler: A Gallery of Ozark Folk Speech*. Norman, OK, 1953.

Rees, Byron. "A Word-List: Chilmark, Martha's Vineyard." *Dialect Notes*, MA, 1917.

Rice, William O. "The Pioneer Dialect of Southern Illinois." *Dialect Notes*, 1902.

Riedel, E. "New Orleans Word-List." *Dialect Notes*, 1916.

Rollins, Hyder E. "A West Texas Word-List." *Dialect Notes*, 1915.

Rontt, James, and Elizabeth Fischer. "Louisiana Gleanings." *Dialect Notes*, 1923.

Routh, James. "Louisiana [Terms]." *Dialect Notes*, 1916–1917.

Ruppenthal, J. C. "A Word-list from Kansas." *Dialect Notes*, 1914–1916.

Ruxton, George F. *Life in the Far West*. Edinburgh, 1849.

Sala, George A. *Gaslight and Daylight, Some London Scenes They Shine Upon*. London, 1859.

Sandilands, John. *Western Canadian Dictionary and Phrase-Book*. Winnipeg, 1913.

Savage, Howard J. "Slang from Bryn Mawr College, 1915–1922." *Dialect Notes*, 1922.

————. "A Word-list from Southwestern Wisconsin." *Dialect Notes*, 1923.

Scargill, M. H. *A Dictionary of Canadianisms on Historical Principles*. Toronto, 1967.

Schele de Vere, Maximilian. *Americanisms: The English of the New World*. New York, 1872.

Shands, H. A. "Some Peculiarities of Speech in Mississippi." *Dialect Notes*, 1893.

Shearin, Hubert G. "An Eastern Kentucky Word-List." *Dialect Notes*, 1911.

Sherwood, Adiel. "Gazetteer of the State of Georgia." *Dialect Notes*, 1837.

Shoemaker, Henry Wharton. *Thirteen Hundred Old Time Words of British, Continental, or Aboriginal Origins, Still or Recently Used Among the Pennsylvania Mountain People*. Altoona, PA, 1930.

Southern Literary Messenger. Richmond, VA, 1845.

Steadman, John. "A North Carolina Word-Book." *Dialect Notes*, 1918–1920.

Stearns, Charles W. *The Shakespeare Treasury: Wisdom and Knowledge*. Philadelphia, 1869.

Stephens, Ann S. *High Life in New York*. London, 1843.

Story, George M. *Dictionary of Newfoundland English*. Toronto, 1982.

Tallman, Marjorie. *Dictionary of American Folklore*. New York, 1959.

Taylor, Jay. "Snake County [Missouri] Talk." *Dialect Notes*, 1923.

Thornton, Richard. *An American Glossary: Being an attempt to Illustrate Certain Americanisms upon Historical Principles* [with supplement]. Philadelphia, 1912.

Trollope, Frances. *Domestic Manners of the Americans*. London, 1832.

Tucker, Gilbert M. *American English*. New York, 1921.

Warnock, Elsie. "Dialect Speech in California and New Mexico." *Dialect Notes*, 1919.

Webster, Noah. *An American Dictionary of the English Language*. New York, 1828.

Wentworth, Harold. *The American Dialect Dictionary*. New York, 1944.

Weseen, Maurice H. *A Dictionary of American Slang*. New York, 1934.

White, Henry Adelbert. "A Word-list from Central New York." *Dialect Notes,* 1912.

Whitney, William D. *The Century Dictionary and Cyclopedia.* New York, 1889.

Williams, John Lee. *A View of West Florida.* Philadelphia, 1827.

Worcester, Joseph. *Dictionary of the English Language.* Boston, 1881.

Wright, Joseph. *The English Dialect Dictionary.* London, 1896–1905.